Taking the Kids to Italy

Memories of a Troubled Trip

Roland Merullo

Taking the Kids to Italy

PFP, INC
publisher@pfppublishing.com
144 Tenney Street
Georgetown, MA 01833

November 2013
Printed in the United States of America

First PFP edition © 2013
ISBN-10: 0989237273
ISBN-13: 978-0-9892372-7-7

(also available in eBook format)

Front Cover Photo:
© Getty Images - David Henderson
"Rolling hills in rural landscape: Italy"

Back Cover Photo:
© Amanda Merullo
Alexandra and Juliana - Acaya, Italy

Also by Roland Merullo

Fiction

Leaving Losapas
A Russian Requiem
Revere Beach Boulevard
In Revere, In Those Days
A Little Love Story
Golfing with God
Breakfast with Buddha
American Savior
Fidel's Last Days
The Talk-Funny Girl
Lunch with Buddha
Vatican Waltz

Non Fiction

Passion for Golf
Revere Beach Elegy
The Italian Summer: Golf, Food and Family at Lake Como
Demons of the Blank Page

Praise for Roland Merullo's Work

Leaving Losapas
"Dazzling . . . thoughtful and elegant . . . lyrical yet tough-minded . . . beautifully written, quietly brilliant."
— *Kirkus Reviews* [starred review]

A Russian Requiem
"Smoothly written and multifaceted, solidly depicting the isolation and poverty of a city far removed from Moscow and insightfully exploring the psyches of individuals caught in the conflicts between their ideals and their careers."
— *Publishers Weekly*

Revere Beach Boulevard
"Merullo invents a world that mirrors our world in all of its mystery . . . in language so happily inventive and precise and musical, and plots it so masterfully, that you are reluctant to emerge from his literary dream."
— *Washington Post Book World*

Passion for Golf: In Pursuit of the Innermost Game
"This accessible guide offers insight into the emotional stumbling blocks that get in the way of improvement and, most importantly, enjoyment of the game."
— *Publishers Weekly*

Revere Beach Elegy: A Memoir of Home and Beyond
"Merullo has a knack for rendering emotional complexities, paradoxes, or impasses in a mere turn of the phrase."
— *Chicago Tribune*

In Revere, In Those Days
"A portrait of a time and a place and a state of mind that has few equals."
— *The Boston Globe*

A Little Love Story

"There is nothing little about this love story. It is big and heroic and beautiful and tragic . . . Writing with serene passion and gentle humor, Merullo powerfully reveals both the resiliency and fragility of life and love . . . It is, quite utterly, grand."
— *Booklist*

Golfing with God

"Merullo writes such a graceful, compassionate and fluid prose that you cannot resist the characters' very real struggles and concerns . . . Do I think Merullo is a fine, perceptive writer who can make you believe just about anything? Absolutely."
— *Providence Journal*

Breakfast with Buddha

"Merullo writes with grace and intelligence and knows that even in a novel of ideas it's not the religion that matters, it's the relationship . . . It's a quiet, meditative, and ultimately joyous trip we're on."
— *Boston Globe*

Fidel's Last Days

"A fast-paced and highly satisfying spy thriller . . . Merullo takes readers on a fictional thrill ride filled with so much danger and drama that they won't want it to end."
— *Boston Globe*

American Savior

"Merullo gently satirizes the media and politics in this thoughtful commentary on the role religion plays in America. This book showcases Merullo's conviction that Jesus' real message about treating others with kindness is being warped by those who believe they alone understand the Messiah."
— *USA Today*

driveway in my two-wheel-drive Camry with its half-bald tires, veering from one snowbank to the next and listening to a sweet-voiced woman on the tape saying: *"Gli Italiani sono molto gentili"*.

"Gli Italiani sono molto gentili" What does it mean, Dad?"

"It means the people in Italy are very kind."

"Are they?'

"Yes, they are," I told her, and that was part of my obsession. I wanted to steep my girls in that particular breed of Mediterranean warmth and *joie di vivre*. Modest, decent, and hardworking as are the inhabitants of the New England countryside, their view of life—in the cold months, at least—can tend toward the hard-bitten and dour. I missed the raucous emotional roller coaster of my youth, the Italian sense of absurd generosity, and the benefits of affectionate physical contact, humor, and food-as-festival. I am not in any way suggesting that Americans can't be warm and festive. Nor am I saying the Italians have no faults. I've seen plenty of warmth in my New England decades, and I know, better even than viewers of that absurd caricature called *Jersey Shore*, the unpleasant aspects of Italian and Italian American culture. Still, as most overseas travelers soon learn, Italy and the Jersey Shore are, well, an ocean apart; there is a relaxed dignity to the Italian style of living (if you don't count the way they drive), and it can serve as the perfect antidote to the fast pace of the American day.

So I trolled the rough waters of the magazine world, fishing for a little paying work on the other side of the Atlantic. Just for fun, I contacted a couple of Italian golf courses and inquired about rates and club rentals.

As we moved deeper into the bleak and pitiless days of January, our financial picture brightened somewhat. Overdue paychecks trickled in, Amanda managed a day or two of photography work—the blooming career she'd given up to be a sworn off teaching by then, though I like teaching, and at one time could even survive, without medication, a night of reading twenty student essays, one or two of which would insist that *Anna Karenina* is a failed novel with qualities similar to the soap opera.

But cold gray day after bitter night, those debts came to seem, by some psychological alchemy, relatively inconsequential. With two hundred dollars in my bank account, and new bills arriving on every one of those days when the mailman could reach the box, I began to send out emails to various Italian contacts, real and fantastical, looking for some means of escape. After the girls were in bed I could be found at the computer on the second floor of the addition Amanda and I built with our own hands, firing off inquiries to real estate agents in Liguria and Sicily, asking about apartments for rent. I'd wake up in the morning, turn on the computer, and, first thing, check the temperature in Rome, Bari, or Genoa, then lift the shade and look out the window at minus ten, or minus four, or plus two and snowing. I called my mother, an upbeat and resilient octogenarian who has traveled with us a dozen times or more, and we started reliving fond memories from past trips. Week by week I worked on Amanda, too, (who, to be honest, didn't need much working on) picking my spots, dropping into our ordinary domestic conversations the memory of a particular Sardinian restaurant in Trastevere, the white wine, the thick lasagna, the magnificent unleavened bread; or a particular stretch of road that ran between mustard fields in Umbria; or a hilltop village in Tuscany where the wine tasted as if the grapes had been grown by angels, harvested by saints, and bottled by monks, mystics, and movie stars.

I started to teach Alexandra—five years old at the time—a few words of the beautiful language I'd heard as a child and studied, intermittently, in college. We'd be skidding down the boldened; they said the same thing now with a knowing smirk. Two kids are more than twice as much work as one, they insisted, *more* than twice as much. The lack of sleep will knock you sideways. The cost of college is going to crush you. Start thinking about Orlando for the week of school vacation . . . if you're lucky. And once they're in school and have friends and commitments—soccer, ballet, algebra II and so on—forget about traveling, just forget about it.

I heard those comments as a personal challenge. We were going to Italy again, soon, and we were going to take the kids. Somehow, where there was the will, there would be the money.

One day in early January the weather eased up: we had sun in the morning, then, in the afternoon, sleet and rain instead of snow. This was followed by a deep freeze which made driving impossible, going for a walk on our road suicidal, and doing anything outdoors with our two young daughters absolutely out of the question. I am by nature an active person—blessing or curse, depending on the situation—and I like to do active things with Alexandra and Juliana, and so this weather-enforced house-arrest was not as workable for me as it might be for a soul who enjoys spending an entire day lying on the couch with a book while the kids play computer games or watch TV. I love books; I'm not opposed to TV, iPods, computer games, and so on. But, strangely perhaps, I do not like being iced in, not in January, with the days short and my spine aching, and the golf clubs gathering dust down cellar.

"It's house arrest," I complained to Amanda, more than once. "In Italy we could be walking around, at least. Going to a playground, kicking a ball."

"Playing golf," she said.

"Playing golf, sure, but that's not why—"

We had debts, I admit that. It's not the most consistently lucrative proposition, making a living writing novels, and I had ing or a curse, depending on the remembered moment in-volved—and, shovelful by shovelful, it was increasingly pleas-urable, as the hours wore on, to recall the feeling of sitting in the 800-year-old cathedral in Lucca with rays of sunlight shin-ing in through the circular stained-glass window above the al-tar; or eating a fabulous six-course meal in a Roman restaurant not listed in any of the guidebooks; or enjoying a picnic lunch of fresh baked bread and strong cheese, with a bottle of chilled white wine in a green pasture with the Dolomites all around us, the sun shining down.

As the winter deepened, so did this use of travel memories as a drug to soften the pain of the bleakness and cold. At breakfast on frigid mornings, I'd look across the table at my wife—who is accustomed to, and often amused by my obses-sion—and say: "I just checked the computer. It's fifty-five in Genoa. Sunny."

"We don't have the money to go to Italy," she'd reply.

"That never stopped us before. Look at all the traveling we wouldn't have done if we'd worried about money."

"We have two little children now, Rol."

That was true. But those kinds of truths have little power over a person whose bones ache from inherited arthritis, who works alone in a room most days, looking out on a frozen landscape, who loves golf and swimming outdoors with his young daughters, and whose predominantly joyful mental equi-librium sometimes tilts beneath the weight of weeks of over-cast skies and the treachery of an icy driveway.

And there was something else going on, besides, a kind of Mediterranean-macho pride reflex that I should confess to right at the start. As mentioned in the prologue, a few of our friends had suggested, when Alexandra was born, that it would be years before we saw Italy again. We immediately proved them wrong. But with the birth of Juliana, they seemed em-

ROLAND MERULLO

without at least half an hour of shoveling, driveway sanding, or windshield scraping. At night, you'd be awakened by what sounded like the well spaced rounds of solitary hunters, but was actually the noise made by exploding tree limbs, their sap freezing solid.

I've lived in New England a long time, all my life in fact, except for a few stints overseas, and I know from a great deal of personal experience that, as they go on and on, winters like this make a person a crazy. Each New Englander's craziness takes a unique form, which is part of the region's charm: some of us seek refuge in drink; some of us go to bed very early and get up very late; some turn on the TV in November and don't turn it off again until May; and in some well insulated homes filled with the quaint smell of burning ash logs, otherwise perfectly decent spouses turn into the husband or wife from hell.

In my case, what happens is that I start thinking about Italy. Not thinking about Italy, exactly, but obsessing about Italy, dreaming about it, talking about it too much at dinners with friends, pulling out old guidebooks and flashcards, combing the Internet, strolling through the kitchen before breakfast saying things like: *"Fa freddo qui, fa troppo freddo"*. On one crisp morning during the early part of that winter, it took me three hours and fifteen minutes to dig my car out from under twenty-six inches of new snow. Unlike some of our neighbors and friends, I actually enjoy shoveling, especially in the silent white stillness that follows a storm. But even for me, three hours seemed an excessively large part of the working day to spend in my driveway, perspiring beneath a wool sweater, puffing out clouds of breath, having to carry each shovelful of soft snow farther and farther afield to find a place to deposit it.

During those hours I found myself replaying happy moments from different trips Amanda and I have made to the *bel paese* the "beautiful land". I have an excellent memory—a bless-

2

1

A thousand feet up in the hills of the western part of Massachusetts, where we live, the first half of the winter of 2003 was unusually cold. There were days when the temperature refused to move out of the single digits. On a few nights it "dipped", as they say around here, to fifteen below.

There is a New England myth that snow doesn't fall in very cold weather, but that year, even before the myth had a chance to be tested, we were buried. The first snowfall arrived in the third week of October, before we'd had time to finish raking the dead oak and maple leaves off the lawn, and it stayed on the ground until the week before Thanksgiving, when we had another storm. By the middle of December there had been two more significant "snow events", as our local meteorologist calls such things, and several "dustings". So much snow piled up that the country road in front of our house turned into a strip of icy tar between parallel mountain ranges of white, and it would not be too much of an exaggeration to say that the danger, in sending small children out to play, was that they might step off the deck and never be heard from again. You couldn't find the mailbox at the side of the road, the trash barrels around back, or the rake you'd left out on the lawn one sunny October Saturday when the trees were red and gold and it seemed the decent weather would stretch out happily, right into the new year. You couldn't leave to go grocery shopping bare-walled motels in the Yucatan, in four-star luxury hotels in Berlin and West Virginia, *zimmers* in Bavaria and on floating Finnish hotel boats on the Neva in what was then called Leningrad. During all these trips we had our share of arguments and disappointments, as travelers do; we contracted intestinal ailments and local influenzas, saw a lot of wonderful landscapes and magnificent architecture, met a number of good people, and had more than our share of fun.

When our first daughter, Alexandra, was born, in 1997, friends with older children counseled us that our traveling days were over, at least until our daughter finished college. So we took her to Lucca, Italy, when she was four months old, just to prove to ourselves that those friends were wrong. We took her and her paternal Grandmother (for some reason, the girls call her "Beetlebah") on a trip to Rome in 2000, and then, when Juliana was born in 2001, we decided to take a short break and travel Stateside until we'd gotten our equilibrium back, gotten used to raising two girls instead of one.

But in the spring of 2003, Italy called to us again, and though we really couldn't afford to go, we went. What follows is the story of that trip, a month in the *bel paese*. It's more than a travelogue, I think, because on this visit to Italy—our seventh in fifteen years—everything that could possibly go wrong, did. We were all tested in different ways. We look back on it now with a sort of wry amusement, and I've tried to present it that way, make it funny, though at the time, in spite of many happy moments, there weren't many laughs to be heard. Long ago I established a personal ritual connected with traveling: before each trip, just as we're about to get on the plane, I say, "the point of this is to learn something about yourself." And on this Italy adventure we all did that.

PROLOGUE

My wife Amanda and I are not wealthy, but we share a great love of travel. We're the kind of people—everyone knows one or two couples like this—who would rather go to Venice, or Moscow, or Guam than have our kitchen cabinets replaced, the living room refurnished, or a new coat of paint applied to old clapboards on the sunny south side of the house. I don't know why this is. I've stopped wondering about it, really. Something in the center of our cells doesn't mind a little peeling paint or a big credit card balance, if it means, for example, that we get to drive a rented car to some mountainside restaurant in Austria and have beer and bratwurst there on the longest day of the year, then sleep beneath a fluffy white quilt in an upstairs room in a stranger's Bed and Breakfast.

Amanda and I were married a long time—eighteen years—without having children. During those years we twice worked for the U.S. Government in the former U.S.S.R., and spent time in eastern and western Europe (including six trips to Italy), Mexico, Canada, and most of the lower forty-eight. My guess is that we drove about a hundred thousand miles on these adventures, including long road trips from Boston to Miami, from Miami to Reno, from Munich to Naples and back. We took trains across Siberia, from Moscow to Berlin, from London to Edinburgh, the hovercraft across the British Channel to Dover, and a bus from Guadalajara to Aquascalientes. We ate *spaghetti al mare*, *huevos rancheros*, shepherd's pie, potato pancakes and pickled herring, and we drank vodka and Beaujolais and Guinness. We swam in the Adriatic and the Black Sea, the Atlantic and the Pacific, Walkensee and Lago di Garda, and waded in Lake Baikal in May. We spent nights in sagging beds in

"Thou Paradise of exiles, Italy!"
Shelly, "Julian and Maddalo"

AUTHOR'S NOTE

As unlikely as it may seem in certain passages, everything written here is true. A few names have been changed to protect privacy; otherwise, this is the way it happened.

In writing this account, I have made use of *Let's Go Italy, 1998*; *Lonely Planet, travel survival kit, Italy*; *Eyewitness Travel Guides, Rome;* and *Guida all' Agriturismo in Italia, 2003*.

For Eileen Merullo, Amanda Merullo, Alexandra Merullo and Juliana Merullo.

The Italian Summer: Golf, Food & Family at Lake Como
"This travel memoir delivers unadulterated joy . . . [Merullo's] account of those idyllic weeks recalls Calvin Trillin in its casual tone, good humor, affable interactions with family, and everyman's love of regional food and wine . . . A special travel book for a special audience."
— *Booklist*

The Talk-Funny Girl
"Merullo not only displays an inventive use of language in creating the Richards' strange dialect but also delivers a triumphant story of one lonely girl's resilience in the face of horrific treatment."
— *Booklist*

Lunch with Buddha
"A beautifully written and compelling story about a man's search for meaning that earnestly and accessibly tackles some well-trodden but universal questions. A quiet meditation on life, death, darkness and spirituality, sprinkled with humor, tenderness and stunning landscapes."
— *Kirkus* [starred review]

Vatican Waltz
"Merullo's latest is a page-turning novel of religious ideas written with love and imagination. . . With fillips of *The Da Vinci Code* conspiracy and *Eat Pray Love* gourmandism, this book will speak loudly to Catholic readers . . .It also sings with finely observed details of family relationships, ethnic neighborhood life, and the life of prayer. The shoulda-seen-it-coming ending is a miracle..."
— *Publishers Weekly* [starred review]

full-time mother.

The weather turned worse and stayed that way. In bed one night we had a long conversation about how best to find some relief from the six-month winter, now, right now, before the girls were enrolled in school full-time and their father was locked in a padded ward fondling his eight-iron and kicking Titleists back and forth across the floor with his bare feet. We decided our more cautious friends were probably right: it was a crazy idea to take a five-year-old and a one-and-a-half-year-old to Italy. What would the girls do for fun over there? How could they make friends without speaking the language? What would the weather be like in late winter? Probably not that much better than it was here. We talked everything over carefully and rationally and decided to go to Florida if we could scrape together the cash. St. Augustine, in fact. We'd stopped through there once, twenty years before, when we were first married, and it seemed like a place worth exploring.

It was settled, then. The next day one of us would start making Internet inquiries about apartments in St. Augustine for the month of February or March. We agreed on that, and went to sleep.

And then, somehow, twenty days later, Amanda and I, Alexandra, Juliana and my mother, were on an Al Italia flight headed east over the Atlantic ocean.

2

The morning after our St. Augustine conversation—not two days later, not a week later, the very next morning—I logged onto the Internet with every intention of doing research on apartments in the Sunshine State. But first I checked my emails. One of the new messages was from a friend in Rome, a kind American woman named Molly from whom we'd rented an apartment two years earlier. She taught art at an American school there, and made absolutely real-looking stones from paper. Her Italian husband, Gino, had led tours through the city for several decades and possessed an encyclopedic knowledge of everything Roman.

Her email was titled: *Return to Italy?* And it went like this:

Dearest Amanda and Roland,

I don't know if you have any interest at all in returning here for another vacation, but I thought I'd let you know that a dear friend of mine, someone I think of as an adopted daughter, has a house to rent an hour and a half northeast of Rome. She would not charge you very much money for it. And it is comfortable for children, and has a beautiful view to the mountains of the interior. Let me know if you are interested.

Coming so close on the heels of our conversation about vacation plans and our decision to go to Florida, this email seemed, to both Amanda and me, like a sign. We do this. Otherwise sensible people, we see the hand of fate in small coincidences. We make decisions, some of them at least, based on chance, hint, fate, the spin of the stars, changes in weather. All through our traveling life, (a life that has taken us to Russia, Uzbekistan, Georgia, Ukraine, Poland, Austria, Switzerland, Germany, Estonia, Lithuania, France, the United Kingdom, Belgium, Slovenia, Mexico, Puerto Rico, Jamaica, Canada, twice across America and six times to Italy) this approach has worked. We never go on organized tours, never make hotel reservations for more than the first night or two. On one trip to Italy, instead of putting together one of our famously loose itineraries before we arrived, we flew to Venice, checked into a hotel, and then adopted the policy of just packing up and walking down to the train station in the morning, looking at the departures board, glancing at a map, and heading off to places we knew nothing about. We were introduced to the mountain city of Merano that way, former vacation spot of Sigmund Freud, with ten-thousand-foot peaks on every side, sixty-cent glasses of excellent red wine, walking trails along the river, impeccably clean hotels with elaborate breakfasts, and an Old World feel. We discovered the little ski town of Vipiteno, near the Brenner Pass, almost in Austria. We went to Verona, on a whim, and loved it. Even the Rome vacation at Molly and Gino's apartment, in 2000, had been based on a chance email from my former agent.

So, as we read over Molly's email together, and then spoke with her friend twice in trans-Atlantic phone calls, we could feel ourselves gradually being drawn away from the city of St. Augustine and toward the country of his birth. We learned that the house that belonged to Molly's friend was in a small city

9

called Contigliano, and this small city, according to our research and our conversations, had all the modern amenities plus a 500-year-old historical section perched on the hill.

Molly followed up her first email with a second one saying the neighbors who lived next to the mountain house were "true, genuine, Italian country folk with hearts of gold."

I make my living from my imagination. It was a healthy dog to begin with, but over the years I've trained it—making up stories, characters, and conversations—so that now it's a muscular Great Dane that can perform all kinds of tricks for me on demand. The problem is, in its free time, the Great Dane gets restless. You can't be making up stories twenty-four hours a day, so in the non-working hours the big pup is running all over the neighborhood pissing on other people's shrubbery, barking at the mailwoman, wandering up into the hills getting itself into trouble chasing skunks and porcupines. Molly's emails, along with one photo of Contigliano I found on the Internet—those things were the equivalent of dripping chunks of raw meat that were leading the Great Dane eastward. I made up a fantasy life. I took scraps of old Italian trips, the sweetest scraps—great meals and superb glasses of wine, architectural treasures, landscapes glimpsed from a passing train, friendly conversations—and stitched them together to make the quilt of a dream life. In my mind's eye I saw the genuine Italian neighbors welcoming us into their home for a meal, making a fuss over our two beautiful girls (every parent loves these fusses), maybe finding a local teenager to babysit while Amanda, my mother, and I played golf at a nearby course. Instead of discouraging it, the gray cold world outside my windows only served to feed this mad dog: the bleaker our present reality, the more vivid our imaginary Italian life became. This is, for me, a kind of minor-league mental illness and over the years I believe I've infected Amanda with it.

We both love golf. After a years of baseball, hockey, rowing, running, and karate, I had settled on golf as the passion of my middle years, and Amanda had taken it up, as well. This meant that I had to endure the jibes of my closest non-golfing friends, who insisted on seeing the game through the filters of their own prejudices, as something invented for the decadent amusement of the ultra rich, as a lazy-man's pastime in which big-bellied retirees scuff up clods of earth and curse and putter around in electric carts while smoking fat cigars and telling bad jokes. But I had fallen in love with the game just about the time Alexandra was born, had made good friends on the fairways, had become reasonably proficient, had even earned some money writing about it for magazines and in two books. My mother, a working-class girl, had been a golfing aficionado for decades, and we'd played together many times. One fine day we took Amanda—a college soccer star and all around fine athlete—with us to a course in New Hampshire. Amanda hit a long straight drive off the first tee—her first golf swing—and she was hooked, too.

So, as the imagination sprinted and barked, and as we did some more research, we found that one of the attractions of the house in Contigliano was its proximity to a small golf course—which I shall refer to here as The Artone Golf Club, though that is a made-up name. On its website, Artone was described as "a challenging and picturesque nine-hole layout with the mountains rising into snow-capped peaks not far from the fairways and greens." I called the *segreteria* of this course and left a message in broken Italian, telling him I sometimes wrote for American golf magazines, and loved the game, and loved Italy, and was renting a house nearby for a month with my family, and we hoped we could play many rounds there. In response, he sent a welcoming, friendly note, full of enthusiasm about our visit.

Shoveling, scraping, putting on and taking off mittens and coats and hats and thermal underwear, slip-sliding down the driveway in winter boots, hoping to find a check in the mailbox, I pictured us there, in Contigliano, striking perfect wedges onto manicured greens, stopping afterwards in a little roadside *trattoria* for a remarkable but simple meal of pasta and wine, with some fresh salad, coffee, a shot of anisette. I imagined us going home to sleep in the mountain house, and waking to the spectacular view, then taking our girls walking through ancient vineyards, world-class museums, sixteenth-century churches, Roman ruins. Perhaps our neighbors would knock on the door at seven a.m. with some fresh milk, goat cheese, peasant bread they'd made with their own hands. Maybe there would be a small property for sale, cheap, needing some work, and I could resuscitate my carpentry skills, turn the place into a European retreat, invite friends over from America, help them escape the harsh winters, too, have my children make Italian friends. Maybe I could even write something about our travel adventure, extend the pleasure to readers unable or unwilling to leave home, or entice others to do what we had done: set those practical concerns aside, ignore the advice of overly cautious acquaintances, pack up the kids, and go.

Those were the types of fantasies that filled my mind in the days before we made the final decision. Really, though, it did not take long to decide. Next to our dreams of Italy, St. Augustine had little chance.

I can't decide where, exactly, to place the responsibility for those dreams. In part, they come from the other trips Amanda and I have taken to the *bel paese*. We've had moments in Italy when life seems to have made impossible promises, and fulfilled them. The country is phenomenally beautiful, with vineyard-covered slopes rising to nine-thousand-foot mountains in the interior, spectacular stretches of sandy and rocky coastline, mediaeval cities perched on the tops of cinnamon-brown hills. Half the world's art treasures can be found in Italy, and even modest provincial museums have collections that include works by great masters—Titian, Tintoretto, Bellini. But, forget the museums, the streets are museums. On our Rome trip, less than three years earlier, the four of us (Juliana had not yet been born) had passed a whole happy month just strolling around the different neighborhoods. For us, walking past a sagging apartment house in the heart of Rome's old Jewish Ghetto, with its thousand-year-old windows and brightly-painted front doors, or stopping into the ethereal space that is the Church of St. Catherine of Siena—that was enough of a reason to go.

And that's before we even start talking about the food. A nutritionist told me once that Italy allows two additives to be legally put into food consumed by humans. America allows two thousand. Italian farms are still mostly small, the food shops still mostly Mom and Pop affairs where the owner feels guilty about offering an overripe piece of fruit or a bad cut of meat. People actually go out of business if they sell you a tomato with skin as hard as a baseball. Chefs are actually embarrassed to overcook pasta before they serve it to you. People eat like you imagine the wild behemoths of Mesopotamia ate in times past . . . and don't carry much excess weight.

And there is great kindness in Italy. Once, on the strength of a three-minute conversation, we were invited to spend the night at the house of a complete stranger, and there were no ulterior motives to the invitation, and we accepted it without hesitation. Men stand up from their tables in outdoor cafes and walk half a block with you to give directions. Grown women and teenage boys and girls compliment you on the attractiveness of your children, on the attempts you make to speak their language. Italians want to please you. Soaked as they are in the warm bath of the sweet life, *la dolce vita*, they want you to get wet, too. They want to show off for you, and showing off sometimes consists of an elaborate Italian generosity.

I blame Italy for my dreams of Italy. And I blame the little trick that travelers play on themselves: remembering the good moments and cultivating a thorough amnesia for the bad. Some very unpleasant things had happened to us on those six previous visits. We'd been cheated by railroad-station hucksters. Harassed by rest-stop con artists offering slightly used car stereos at rock-bottom prices. Buried in paperwork and impossibly intricate rules by ticket clerks and low-echelon officials. In the Italian countryside, you see African prostitutes standing by the side of the road, flagging down men in cars at the risk of being beaten, infected with HIV, or killed. On the highways you meet Mario Andretti wannabes, pulling up to within an inch of your bumper at ninety miles an hour. Often, the policemen you approach when you are lost and in need of help, appear to feel it is beneath them to give directions. The waiters don't want to serve you when the official lunch hour (noon to three) is over. The women in snack bars make you a desultory cappuccino in late afternoon (because you cannot be served at that hour in the restaurant next door) with about as much enthusiasm as if you've asked them to wash out three pairs of your old socks.

But those things are forgotten. Or, if not forgotten, they are turned into amusing anecdotes for your more financially responsible friends back home. They become the mole on Sophia Loren's cheek. What remains is the memory of the architectural masterpieces along the Venetian canals, the taste of a particular glass of Bardolino from a ten-dollar bottle you bought at a supermarket in Monteverde Nuovo, a dish of *spaghetti al pesto* on the Ligurian coast, a mustachioed, middle-aged man waving his arms like a ballet dancer as he tells a joke to a friend in the Padua railroad station, the warm, green-gray waves of a beach on the Adriatic, the pocked pillars of the Roman Forum, the sculptures of Florence, the rugged shapes of the Dolomites, an emerald-green field of tall grass four thousand feet above sea level not far from Gran Sasso, a curl of shore at Santa Margherita Ligure with olive trees above the cliffs.

You are seduced. Your sleep-deprived brain feels the warm syrup of Italian memories flow over it and nothing matters then, not concerns about money, health, or pipes freezing back home in Massachusetts. Nothing matters, nothing. You are going back.

After one last husband-and-wife conversation, I told Molly's friend we'd take the house for the month of February. I wrote out and mailed the deposit check. Called my mother and told her to put a suitcase together; she was coming with us on another Italian adventure. Amanda made the airline reservations and started making a list of things we'd need to bring. Suddenly, the harsh New England winter had lost some of its force.

3

Our Italian vacation began with a smooth Al Italia flight from Logan Airport in Boston to Malpensa in Milan. Fairly smooth. Reasonably smooth. Amanda loves flying. It appeals to her finely developed visual sense, and she's such a travel-nut that even the drive to the airport makes her happy. I love traveling, too, but I despise flying. It's not fear so much as the feeling that, in bringing our bags up to the check-in desk we are putting signatures on an invisible document that allows us to be turned into so many heads of cattle in the stockyard: subservient, mutely suffering, moved from one enclosure to the next on route to some fate over which we have no control. I felt this way even before September 11, 2001. Since then it's a hundred times worse, naturally, and going through the whole security ritual I always think of those nineteen hijackers, the insane-making anger they must have felt to be able to do what they did, the egotism and absurdity of believing that God is instructing you to kill innocent people, destroy families, terrorize a nation, and will be eternally proud of you for murdering children. I said to a golfing friend of mine the next day, when we were playing a round under eerily empty skies: "Nothing will ever be the same now, in this country." And, of course, nothing is. Nineteen bastards with box cutters, and they left a legacy of pain and paranoia as large and long-lasting as any rampaging army.

For our family, which lost no one on that day, the legacy boils down to inconvenience, nothing more. Inconvenience that sours what ought to be an exciting moment. The security personnel at Logan Airport studied our baggage as if, in its lumpy, dusty, scratched-up form it somehow reflected the state of our souls. Take off your shoes, your coat, empty your pockets, pass through an X-ray machine, then sit and wait and wait, listening to tape recorded announcements and sneezing fellow passengers before you're shepherded through an airless tunnel, squeezed into a metal tube in the bowels of which disenchanted workers are slamming your golf clubs about. Turned into animals themselves, your fellow passengers elbow their way down the aisle, or stop to force leather lumps (reflections of the state of their souls?) into too-small overhead compartments designed to pop open in rough weather and drop these lumps down on unsuspecting neighbors. People cheat, take the wrong place on purpose, badger the flight crew for a window seat, an aisle seat, a blanket or a pillow or a cup of water so they can take their anti-vomiting medication before it's too late. They slap you in the eye with the leather belt of a raincoat, burp, jostle, talk to you about television shows you haven't seen and don't care to see, pretend not to be nervous at takeoff and landing.

Strapped in place, engines whistling and whining, the captain greeting you in a soothing contralto with a Midwestern accent, you are read a set of instructions on water landings and drops in cabin pressure, made to watch videos of well-dressed mothers calmly putting masks over their own faces and, only then, tending to their absolutely un-panicked children. You rush down the runway at an unnatural speed, the cabin shaking, compartment doors flapping, a child wailing, a neighbor chattering. And then you fly.

What's not to like?

I enjoy it so little, in fact, that I encourage Amanda (who usually makes the travel arrangements) to take great pains to arrange for us to fly direct whenever possible, and so avoid the further aggravation of changing planes. If I have to fly, I want to get on the plane, endure what I have to endure, and get off at my destination. One takeoff, one landing, and then at least a full month before I see another airport lounge.

This little quirk of mine makes travel plans more complicated. And making them more complicated still, in this instance, was the fact that, since our last trip, in late winter of 2000, Al Italia had moved its hub from Rome to Milan, so most international flights are routed through that northern city. With two young children and our golf clubs and stroller, it made more sense to fly to Milan, and just get off the plane and drive south to Contigliano, rather than fly to Milan, get off the plane with two jet-lagged little girls, wait around, get on another plane, fly to Rome, and then have to drive north from Rome to Contigliano anyway. Made sense to me, at least, even though as Amanda pointed out, more than once, Contigliano was a two-hour drive north from Rome, but a two-day drive south from Milan.

We'd see more of the country if we did it my way, I argued. Show the girls a swath of northern Italy. Avoid the traffic madness of the capital.

Amanda and I have learned, during all our travels, during all our many years of marriage, to indulge, or at least try to indulge, the other person's quirks. Probably, I deserve some credit for pushing us out the door more than once when it would have been prudent not to spend the money. We've had some nice times because of that. And probably Amanda deserves a lot of credit for putting up with a traveling partner who hates airports and cheap hotels, and gets blinded by his enthusiasms—especially in winter—whisking the family off to places we haven't ever seen, on the strength of a fantasy, a phone call, an email photo or two.

But it was a smooth flight, really, a silk napkin laid across a flat table with small ruffles at either end, a bump or two at takeoff and near landing. Amanda and I had worried that seven-and-a-half hours on a jet would be too much for the girls, or for my eighty-year-old mother. But my mother, or "Beetlebah", is tough as nails beneath an upbeat, obliging exterior, tempered by the Depression and by military service as a physical therapist in World War II. And Alexandra and Juliana handled it perfectly. Or almost perfectly. Just before takeoff Amanda gave them each a dose of Benadryl, that well known, harmless, over-the-counter allergy medication said to encourage sleep. Something went wrong. Juliana dozed for a while after the meal was served (and on Al Italia a meal actually is served: decent cut of beef with smoked salmon on the side and a small bottle of red wine) then woke up and spent the next three and a half hours climbing over her mother in the fashion made popular by baby chimpanzees, all the while yelling at top volume: "Up on Mommy! UP! UP!"

Over Mommy's mild objections, Alexandra was allowed to watch the film *Sweet Home Alabama*. By the time the movie started, she was two hours past her bedtime, but even then she was a curious child, older than her years, and she plugged in the plastic earphones and worked hard to make sense of what was happening on the screen. When the film ended, somewhere in the early morning hours, mid-Atlantic, she, too, settled down for her Benadryl-aided sleep. She lay her head on my lap and pushed her feet up near the darkened window. No good. Legs too long. She sat up, shushed her sister—one row in front, still clambering up and around, tirelessly—and tried again, laying her head against the thrumming side of the aircraft and kicking me repeatedly in a loving and mostly accidental way. Also no good: Dad objected to being kicked. She shushed her sister again, less patiently. She moved and squirmed and sighed and eventually, more than half a night past her bedtime, fell asleep, leaning against me so that I was obliged, good father that I am, to remain as still as a yoga master in meditation. Juliana eventually settled down. My mother and Amanda dozed. The flight was half-full, so some of the other passengers, dignified grown men and women, stretched out across the empty rows with blankets over their torsos, mingling their private grunts and groans with the steady drone of the 767's engines.

But there were no other empty seats, and, like a lot of other people, I cannot fall asleep sitting up—another reason to dislike flying. So I sat there, barely moving, surrounded by loved ones, absolutely wide awake, full of dreams of Italy.

4

There are one or two bumps as we glide down over the sharp, snowy peaks that separate Switzerland from Italy, and then a smooth landing in Malpensa, and then we are staggering tiredly around the baggage claim area trying to figure out how to work the self-locking device where the luggage carts stand in neat rows. Cash doesn't seem to work, credit cards don't seem to work. The kids are scampering here and there, and I feel as though there are wet wool blankets hanging across my brain, the word "sleep" echoing there like an airport terminal announcement. Sleep. Sleep. Sleep. Passenger Merullo, arriving on Al Italia flight 576 from Boston, please go to the information counter immediately and sleep.

The carts are secured, in some mysterious fashion, to a chest-high metal box. We jiggle the box, bang on it, slip a credit card in and out six or seven times, and then, finally, come to understand that the machine accepts only a certain Euro coin, minted since our last visit. At a painful commission, we manage to coerce a few of these coins out of another, larger metal box that swallows dollars, and then we manage to free two metal carts. Someone in the group is awake enough to do the math: eighteen of our nineteen bags are accounted for. The missing piece of luggage is the black canvas bag that holds my golf clubs—a beautifully-made set of forged Hogan irons with graphite shafts, a putter I won at a tournament named after my

21

late father, and a classic old driver that once belonged to the Commandant of the Marine Corps and had been given to me by his son. I am not someone who cares very much about things; that bag of metal sticks is an exception.

Alexandra and I go striding about the cluttered linoleum floor of the claim area, trying the closed doors of various offices, poking at various piles of abandoned-looking, odd-shaped pieces of luggage: cardboard boxes tied with yarn, old leather trunks, knapsacks that should have been sent to Sydney or Ouagdougou. That whole section of the baggage claim area is a sort of dog pound for bags that will soon either be donated to some needy group, or euthanized.

A tired mind is prone to negativity, and as we make our unsuccessful search, it occurs to me, through the haze of exhaustion, that the name Malpensa can be broken down into *mal* —which means "bad" in Italian, and "*pensa*" which comes from the verb *pensare* "to think". A bad thought. Bad thinking. Badly thought out. Maybe we should have flown to Rome instead, as Amanda suggested. The golf clubs are missing, the Benadryl didn't work, the Great Dane is angry now and turning on its master . . . but then Alexandra spies another sad pile of bags near the door to The Office of Odd Shaped Pieces, and we find the clubs there, apparently unharmed, the white tag with my name on it clearly declaring ownership.

All children accounted for. All baggage accounted for. As I am rolling the awkward golf bag toward another room that seems to have an exit door, Alexandra holding onto one sleeve, Amanda pushing the luggage cart, and my mother pushing Juliana in the stroller, into our blood goes a jolt of travel narcotic, a familiar dose of pure joy that comes from being in a new place. All compulsive travelers feel this; it is what keeps us flying. The unusual smells, the different-looking advertisements in a foreign language; the people around us speaking another tongue (they seem dressed differently, seem to move different-ly); even the airport landscape beyond the windows, gray, in-dustrial, and unattractive though it is, strikes our eyes in a fresh way. This is another part of the human experience, and you are about to have the privilege of seeing, smelling, hearing, touch-ing, and tasting it. The girls are excited, without exactly know-ing why. The uniformed customs agents, lined up next to a ta-ble, lounging, gabbing, laughing, take one look at them and wave us casually through, as if it is a law of this new universe that any couple who has somehow managed to produce such creatures cannot possibly be smuggling anything improper into the Republic of Italy.

Pushing the overloaded trolleys in front of us, we move out of the customs zone and into the terminal itself, where the sounds of squeaking luggage carts and kids' voices echo against the vaulted ceiling. There is an exchange office there. I change some more money at the usual usurious rate, and hand half of it over to Amanda. Even that small thing—the feel of Euro notes in our hands—makes us strangely happy. My mother is alternately watching the kids and studying the newness and freshness of everything. Amanda is smiling tiredly, and she has a smile you'd marry her for. After a minute or two of this, we locate a pay telephone (these are pre-cell phone days, at least for most Americans), which looks like an overloaded orange metal knapsack screwed to the wall, and call our friend Valter at Renault.

Valter is not really a friend, though we think of him that way even now. Before that morning at Malpensa, in fact, we had never met him. Surfing the Internet one night, Amanda discovered that Renault had a program (since discontinued) where, instead of renting a car from them for the month, you leased it, became the owner for the length of your vacation. This deal had some advantages over the ordinary rental situation: in addition to there being no limit to the amount of miles you could drive, you had full insurance coverage, and all licensed drivers were allowed behind the wheel. And the price tag was surprisingly modest. After looking over the various options on the Renault homepage—European thimbles on wheels—we'd decided on a model called the Kangoo, which *seemed*—I emphasize this word—to have enough cubic feet of storage space to hold our hundred and four thousand pounds of absolutely necessary luggage. ("You're in trouble then," my friend Peter said, over the phone, when I told him about our choice. "Driving something called a "Kangoo" in Italy. You're already in trouble.")

Amanda liked the Renault deal but worried the Kangoo wouldn't be big enough. There were some statistics included on the page where the car was described, and we spent a couple of fruitless hours trying to figure out what 3.4 cubic meters of space looked like. It was a legitimate worry on her part because we always say we're going to pack light this time, then end up packing like the Allied Army preparing for its march across Europe. My golf clubs (Amanda put her putter, driver, five-iron and wedge into the bag), the stroller, the portable crib, the bushels of diapers, wet-wipes and lotions, medicines for every eventuality, changes upon changes of clothes, books, laptops, cameras, flashlights, shoes, boots and sneakers, pads of paper, pens, one set of fancy clothes, heavy coats, light coats, favorite dolls, children's games, etc. etc. Amanda tends to be the practical half of the pair. This is a good thing that can occasionally mutate into a bad thing. For instance, at one point in the worried preparations, she suggested I leave my golf bag at home.

But the golf bag is there with us, safe, along with everything else, and when I dial Valter's number from the phone inside the terminal, he answers immediately—which strikes us as a positive sign. In those days my telephone Italian was shaky at best, but, after asking him to repeat himself a couple of times, I believe I understand Valter to say he will meet us outside the terminal in five minutes. I pass the message on to my fellow adventurers. We gather ourselves, trying to keep the luggage from tipping off the carts, and step out into the surprisingly cool Italian morning. No snow at least, but surprisingly, disturbingly cool. We've spent all this money and come all this way because Italy promised to be warmer than Massachusetts . . . and it is, but not much warmer. It must be, we decide, that the sun hasn't yet risen high enough to take away the chill of the night air.

Valter is as good as his word. Small, nervous, friendly, bearing that bemused impatience you see in Germanic peoples stationed in Italy, he hurries up to us on the sidewalk outside the terminal and points over his shoulder at a green vehicle that is nice-looking but somehow smaller and narrower than it appeared on the computer screen. Our Kangoo. I look down at the two bulging luggage carts, look up at the boxy back of the Kangoo, and wonder, for just the tiniest moment, if it might have been wiser to leave the golf clubs at home.

While Beetlebah keeps an eye on the girls—a bit of pent-up energy there after the long flight—Amanda and I open the back of the Kangoo and make an assessment. Valter watches us optimistically and offers encouraging noises. Like people attempting to solve an oversized Rubick's Cube, we try different ways of squeezing the bags into the Kangoo. After several failed configurations, we find one that works. Nineteen bags in and the door closes! No matter that everyone but the driver will have to use up lap space; no matter that the driver will not be able to see through the rear-view mirror; no matter that, as we will learn later, this is the only configuration that allows all our bags to fit—any small deviation from the plan and we'll end up with something important left on the sidewalk. The point is that they fit then, at that moment, perfectly, or almost perfectly. Valter is happy for us. He shows us how to turn on the lights, the wipers. He jots down the number of a friend who works in a nearby hotel where we can stay at a discount on the night before our flight home, one month from now. He asks us to sign twelve pieces of paper we can't really read, the technical mumbo-jumbo of legalese compounded by the fact that it is in a language we speak poorly. He gives us directions that, between the two of us, we almost understand. He shakes our hands, smiles, wishes us well, and we are in Italy.

We all squeeze into the Kangoo, buckle up, align the mirrors, and putter off, away from the terminal, telling each other what a nice man Valter is and what a good deal we've stumbled upon. We've gone less than a kilometer when I notice that the needle of the gas gauge stands on empty.

Five minutes further down the road we stop for fuel and a coffee-and-brioche breakfast in a gas station snack bar. There is something especially nice about this humble roadside cafe: the smell of espresso and steamed milk, the ambience of leisure one finds in almost every Italian eating place—no rush there, no stress. But some of the customers are smoking, and the smoke soon chases Amanda and the girls out the door and in the direction of the WC around back. My mother and I, non-smokers both but a bit more tolerant of tobacco, have a pleasant moment together, standing at the tall table sipping from our cups. I don't remember what we talk about, but, like Amanda, both of us have a talent for appreciating the small things in life: the heft of the coffee cup, the chocolately macchiato, the dough of the brioche in our fingers, the difference of everything. We linger there for two or three minutes, sipping and eating, studying a few pretty coins on the tabletop, and the newspaper headlines announcing impending war in Iraq. We make a little tired small talk. "Are you going to be awake enough to drive?" my mother wants to know.

I blink, force my eyelids up, take a gulp of the super-test macchiato. "Of course, Mum." I say. "Naturally."

She smirks.

We finish our snack and thank the waitress and go outside, where we hear a report that the toilets in the WC *do not even have any seats*, Dad!

In the Kangoo, the girls sleepily rearrange themselves, get out workbooks and dolls, buckle seatbelts.

I settle in, too . . . and turn on the heat, because the morning is surprisingly cold.

5

Let me make the immodest claim that, as far as driving a car in Italy goes, I am a past master. This expertise is hard-earned, having come from a month of piloting a wide-hipped Rover sedan through the serpentine streets of Rome, and, before that, driving from Trieste to Naples and back—a distance of several thousand miles—in a Ford Escort. True, on one sunny Roman morning there was a single-car-accident type of moment with the Rover, which I probably shouldn't get into. And, true, the diminutive Ford Escort proved capable of exceeding 100 m.p.h., which I also probably shouldn't get into. But, as I'm sure Amanda will agree, neither of those facts has any real bearing on my driving mastery of the Italian roads.

In the past decade I have logged at least ten thousand miles on Italy's Interstates (called *Autostradas*), on her two-lane country highways, side roads, dirt roads, and narrow, fifteenth-century alleys. And I can say this: the Italians are excellent drivers. They have to be.

They have to be because the first rule of the Italian road is that there are no rules (Dave Barry puts it in a different way: he says that the first and only rule is: you cannot be behind somebody). In the great Italian tradition, rules would imply government interference in the lives of private citizens, and that would not be well tolerated. Obeying such rules would smack of a sissified subservience, a gullibility, an admission that there might actually be a legitimate governmental authority to which one ought to pay some regard. Stopping at red lights in modern Italy has become a gesture of *politesse*, one of several options. Crossing solid lines to pass a slower vehicle, preferably on the curve of a mountain road, is a requirement for every Italian man—and, now, most Italian women—before they are allowed to engage in sexual activity for the first time. Buses swoop into the opposite lane to navigate impossible corners on switchback mountain roads because to do otherwise, to slow down for instance, or to stay on their own side of the solid line, would be a sign of the driver's lack of faith in a benevolent and protective Creator. It is no accident, to use an unfortunate turn of phrase, that Italy has produced some of the world's greatest race cars and race car drivers, that it has one of the highest motor vehicle fatality rates in Europe, or that there are thousands of small private shrines to various saints set up along the roadsides from Sicily to the Alps.

Once, not far from the city of Asti, I was driving west on a two-lane highway, going fifty-five or so. Another car was coming east. There was a solid line between us. We were separated—our front bumper to theirs—by perhaps a hundred yards. Ninety yards. Eighty yards. A driver pulled up fast behind me and, without the smallest hesitation, straddled the solid line so that I was encouraged—to use a nice word— to move my right wheels over to within inches of the gravel shoulder, and the approaching car was obliged to do likewise on the opposite side. The passing driver moved between us with a hand's width to spare and went along happily up the road toward the next encounter. He could have waited probably fifteen seconds and passed without worrying about or in any way inconveniencing the oncoming car, but that would have been boring, cowardly, unmanly and un-Italian.

Here is the key: the Italians' definition of a close call is different than ours. This may be because many of them grow up

29

in apartments rather than suburban homes and they are accustomed to tighter quarters. It may be because they are, on average, slightly smaller than Americans. It may be because they feel especially well-protected by God.

Whatever the reason, it is common, on the Autostrada, to glance in the rear-view and see only an empty lane behind, then glance back three seconds later and see a Lancia or BMW or sometimes a Maserati a few inches from your bumper, lights flashing impatiently, driver gesturing with one hand and holding a cell phone to his ear with the other, steering with his knees. You move into the slow lane, going seventy-five, and the Lancia passes as if you are standing still. Four seconds later it is out of sight.

In the cities, in Rome and Naples especially, this close-quarters maneuvering is made immeasurably more complicated by the thousands of buzzing motor scooters or *motorini* that dart in and out of traffic. Change lanes too quickly and you run the risk of causing serious bodily harm—possibly to the child riding there on the front of the *motorini*, helmetless, between his father's knees. So, caution is required. But if you are too cautious, you will be devoured.

In case the picture is not clear, let me cite one last example, which stands in my mind as the Ultimate Italian Driving Moment. Before we had children, Amanda and I spent a little time in Trento, a stony, foreboding, interesting city northwest of Venice. After our visit, we left Trento on a commuter bus, climbing a two-lane mountain highway, headed north. We were sitting by the window about midway back on the driver's side, looking left across the southbound lane, over the guard rail, and down a thousand or so feet into a picturesque valley of tidy homes and vineyards. Though there was a solid line between the two lanes, a BMW crossed it and moved up beside us, squarely in the other lane, going the wrong direction. Nothing especially unusual there, though the bus was moving along at a good clip; you occasionally see such things even in Massachusetts. But then, as if in a gesture of compound impatience, or exponential daring, a tiny, much less powerful Fiat moved up beside the BMW—going the wrong way *in the breakdown lane on the other side of the road, uphill, one arm's length away from the guard rail and the thousand-foot drop*—and passed the BMW and the bus. Two seconds after the lane was clear, a tractor-trailer loaded with timber came hurtling down the highway, shaking the sides of the bus.

So, with this in mind, on a night of zero sleep, after confidently assuring my mother of my road-competence, I buckle my seatbelt, look around at my beloved females, square my shoulders, put the Kangoo in gear, and we are on the road.

6

The land around Milan is one of the few unattractive parts of the Italian peninsula, somehow fertile and ugly at the same time, with long stretches of flat farmland broken only by the occasional cement plant or high-tension wire. Soon after we leave the gas station/coffeeshop, Juliana falls asleep, then Alexandra. In another hour we reach the outskirts of Parma—the home of Stendahl, Verdi, and Toscanini and the birthplace of Parmesan cheese—a city I have long wanted to visit. We decide not to visit it on this trip, to let sleeping children lie. We turn west onto A-15, and speed down the western slopes of the Apennines toward a city called La Spezia, moving from Italy's mountainous middle toward its western coast, gliding from an altitude of 5,000 feet down to sea level. This is the same mountain pass Hannibal led his elephants and men through, after he decided to head south along the Ionian Sea instead of advancing directly on the defenses of Rome. Napoleon took this route into the interior, going the opposite direction. And a friend's mother, born and raised here and now living in America, walked from Parma to La Spezia—fifty miles—during the war because she knew she could get some salt in La Spezia.

The hillsides to either side of the famous valley are brown and gray, the air smoky from grapevine cuttings being burned at the edges of small vineyards. As we descend toward the coast we see a few patches of snow on the higher hills and in the shaded spots, and though this does not exactly square with our dreams of Italy, with the idea that it simply *must* be warm in this country at this time of year, we drive happily on. True, the air was colder than expected at the airport. But isn't Milan up on a plateau? True, that seems to be more snow there in the shaded places by the road. True, when we open the window for bursts of fresh air it feels remarkably cool, but we tell ourselves it will definitely be warmer where we're going, it has to be.

We drop down to the coast in great A-15 swoops, turn south, and pass the city of Carrara. As the Romans did before him, Michelangelo had his marble quarried here because he thought it was the best marble on earth, and he traveled more than once to Carrara to personally select various pieces. Hundreds of years after his death, the hillsides are still being harvested, the quarries looking like jagged white scars shining in the sun. The girls are awake by now, and so, just after noon we stop in Pietrasanta (the name means "sacred stone"), a small, pleasant city where an American friend is working on a documentary about weddings. We make a phone call, but our friend is unable to leave the set and join us for lunch, so we park the loaded Kangoo in what we hope is a safe area, break out the stroller, and make our way along Pietrasanta's cobblestone streets. The kids are hungry after their naps. We are all hungry.

The first restaurant we come upon looks wonderful. Unfortunately, half the population of Pietrasanta thinks so, too. No empty seats. No place to park a stroller. We walk on. The second and third restaurants we pass are closed. This is Thursday, one p.m., Italy, and it makes no sense that the restaurants should be closed, but they are. At last, hidden on a side street, we find a place that is called, for some reason, Trattoria Ski. We squeeze in the door like a small invading army, occupy a strategically positioned corner booth, and are served a fine lunch of bread, salad, and *pasta al pomodoro* which the girls do not touch. At home, they ask for pasta every night (recently Alexandra has decided she will ask only every other night); here, in the home of pasta, they don't touch it. The good news is that the toilets have seats, the bad news that our neighbors are smoking.

At a nearby table a man is sleeping sitting up, a skier perhaps, depressed by the approaching end of winter and the lack of slopes for scores of miles in any direction. An empty bottle of wine stands in front of him. Near the end of the meal the waitress tells us that Trattoria Ski does not accept credit cards because she doesn't know how to work the machine. Only the boss, her husband—she gestures to the sleeping drinker—knows how to work the machine and he is, well, you can see what he is. I pay in cash and ask for a receipt (because of an assignment I conjured from a golf magazine, a small part of the trip will be tax deductible), but she informs me that she doesn't know exactly how to write out receipts. "Here," she says, gesturing kindly to the pad of paper beside the cash register, "write out your own receipt if you like." So I do that.

Outside, in the sunny town square, we watch seven men watching two men work, replacing paving stones. In part because Alexandra loves to light votive candles, in part because my mother is a devout Catholic, in part because I love Italian churches, we stop into the sixteenth-century church for a prayer. There, inside, we discover another Italy, ancient and echoing, smelling of cool stone and candle wax, light streaming in through stained glass; black, white, and brown marble altars, improbably perfect columns and stone curlicues, old chestnut pews, the smudge and blood and gleam of history, a few local women at prayer. In two steps we have walked backwards into the mysteries of ancient Europe, escaping the modern turmoil of the war preparations, the cigarette smoke, the highway frenzy, and joining ourselves to the whole long, mottled history of religious belief, the whole sense that there is something greater, something larger, something finer than our pain-spotted earthly life. In a way, it's a similar idea that has drawn me back to Italy, as if life is somehow larger and finer here, warmer, as if I can more easily touch some better version of me.

7

But, alas, this better version of me is not exactly how I would describe the person behind the wheel as we head out of Pietrasanta. The Mediterranean coastline is wreathed in smoke from burning grapevine cuttings, and, after thirty-six hours without sleep I am as tired as a circus hand at the end of summer. So we get lost going out of town because we carefully follow signs to the Autostrada and those signs lead us straight into the parking lot of a train station. So what? We'd gotten lost going into Pietrasanta, as well, for similar reasons. We'd had that kind of trouble with signs in southern France, too, and come to the conclusion that, descended from a long line of masterful artists as they are, Italian and French road crews, like Italian and French drivers, want to have some creativity in their lives. They don't like the idea of being constrained by the actual rules of the road, or the actual routes their signs are supposed to indicate. The automobile was not designed to be driven at regular speeds in straight lines. And road signs are not meant simply to replace the pointed finger. What matters is setting them in such a way, at such an angle, that they catch the right kind of light at a certain time of day in a particular season and, like all great art, encourage one to contemplate the magnificence of being alive. The fact that they might mislead visiting tourists is less than secondary.

In the weeks leading up to the trip, as I always do before

our vacations to Italy, I took some sandpaper to my rusty Italian. My command of the language is absolutely strong enough to enable me to ask directions, though, unfortunately, or *sfortunatamente*, not always strong enough to enable me to understand the directions once they are given. It's a famously beautiful, but surprisingly challenging language, and, when in Italy, Amanda and I practice it every chance we get. So, in the parking lot of the Pietrasanta train station, where we have inadvertently ended up, I inquire of a fresh-faced, black-haired young man, sitting on the curb with his backpack beside him, as to the best way to the Autostrada. Like every un-uniformed Italian we have ever approached for roadside help, he is happy to be of assistance. The directions to the highway are very simple, he says—we'd almost made it on our own—and he gives them to us in clear, basic Italian. We respond with *grazies* from both the front and back seats, and soon we can hear the roar of engines that tell us the Autostrada is near.

Though the air cannot yet be called warm, it at least looks warm from inside the car. As we merge onto the Autostrada and rumble along at seventy-five miles an hour, Amanda, my mother, and I remark, in a grateful, optimistic way, on the absence of snow, the patches of green, the strong sunlight refracting through sweet-smelling smoke. The Autostrada itself is in beautiful condition—building and maintaining roads is something the Italians do very well— and we cruise happily along with green and gray mountains to our left, glimpses of the Mediterranean to our right, speeding Lamborghinis, rumbling eighteen-wheelers, exorbitant tolls (that fund highway maintenance), rows of grapevines and tile-roofed stone farmhouses on the hills. The girls whine and fidget a bit and exclaim and play games with my mother, who is sitting between them. Amanda, who has no Italian blood whatsoever, says, "It feels like we've come home."

As the dinner hour approaches, we have been driving for most of a day and have made it about halfway to our mountain home in Contigliano, so we are right on schedule. At a bathroom-and-coffee pit stop, we see from the map that we're not far from the city of Lucca, one of Napoleon's favorite places and also one of ours. Amanda and I have good memories of that first big trip we ever made with Alexandra, to Lucca, when she was four months old. It's a walled city, one of Italy's wealthiest, with excellent restaurants, a spectacular twelfth-century cathedral that houses Tintoretto's *Last Supper*, modern shops, a Roman amphitheater, and friendly, sophisticated, extraordinarily well-dressed people.

So when I spy the word LUCCA on our map, another dream-image comes to me, similar to the one that brought us to Italy in the first place. The image spawns an idea: Rather than finding two rooms in a hotel somewhere, and having to unload all our luggage and carry it up three flights of stairs, only to have to carry it down again the following morning; rather than trying to enter the city itself, where parking is tightly controlled, we will find a country inn, or *agriturismo*, and spend the night there. Most *agriturismos* have a restaurant on the premises. Staying at an *agriturismo* will free us of the need to get the girls out of and then back into their car seats, drive around looking for a place to park, a place to eat that looks suitable, and so on. The food at these *agriturismos* is usually very good, too, a mix of hearty country fare and gourmet cuisine, with fresh produce, homegrown meat, local wines and olive oil, all of it finished off with homemade liqueurs served by friendly hosts. We'll find one of these *agriturismos*, have a memorable three or four-course dinner, then just climb a flight of stairs and fall, at last, into a comfortable sleep.

I have a strong intuition that there will be an especially wonderful *agriturismo* somewhere near Lucca. Prompted by that vision, and with Amanda's consent, I leave the Autostrada and work the Kangoo along secondary highways, south and a bit west. By that point, the strain of the trans-Atlantic crossing has caught up with all of us. We are hungry again, and the girls are exhausted, understandably whiney, fidgety, asking where we're going and when we'll be there and if they can eat this or that from the snack bag. One of them keeps kicking the back of the driver's seat in mute protest. My mother taught middle school for twenty-five years, and is an expert at finding ways—songs, card games, word games, jokes and riddles—of calming this kind of youthful uprising. But even her talents can't quite put a lid on the simmering dissatisfaction in the back seat. It isn't easy, trying to drive or navigate with all this going on. With increasing urgency, Amanda and I search the clutter of roadside signage for the familiar brown and yellow rectangle with AGRITURISMO on it. There has to be one close by. I am as sure that there has to be one, as I'd been sure Italy would be warm in February. Lucca is a prosperous city, so many tourists visiting, such nice landscape nearby with the rolling hills and stucco villas, gardens and orchards, vineyards and churches, all squeezed between the ocean and the hills. There has to be an *agriturismo* in those parts.

But there isn't. We drive and drive. The girls' fidgeting evolves from subtle to obvious to desperate. Every few minutes Amanda has to turn around in her seat to quell some border skirmish being fought across the front of my mother's body. Juliana's vocabulary is limited, but her lungs are strong. She is tired of being strapped into a seat, all her freedom taken away by bigger, stronger autocrats, and she expresses this complex idea by straining against the shoulder belt and shouting, "UP ON MOMMY! UP! UP!" at top volume. I worry about her, about Alexandra, about my mother—eighty years old, hadn't slept well on the plane, had left a comfortable house near Boston to come with us on this "adventure" as I'd described it to her, more than once. "We've rented a house with a great view in the hills," I told her over the phone, though we'd seen the house in Contigliano only on a handful of email pictures. "It's close to where Saint Francis used to live, not far from Assisi, and some other beautiful cities: Orvieto, Spoleto, Perugia. There's a nice little golf course there, I've done some research on it, I called the other day. Open year round. The weather will be in the fifties, maybe sixties by the time we've been there a while. We'll have some good meals, see some churches, play some golf, get away from the winter."

"Oh, I'm not sure," she said, more than once.

I kept pressing, throwing out glowing descriptions from the guide books and travelogues.

So, wrapped in guilt and tiredness, the negative winds blowing hard through the fields of my mind, I say things like: "There has to be an agri around here, has to be. I feel it."

But there isn't. We search and search, hungry, tired, crankier by the minute. A cool but sweet, late-winter dusk is dropping its gauzy curtain down over southern Europe. We are close to Lucca by then, just on the outskirts. I pull over on the side of a busy road, jog across its two lanes, and approach a gas station attendant with this question: *"Ci sono gli agriturismi qui vicino?"* Any agriturismos hereabouts? He turns to look at me as if his ex-wife had cheated on him multiple times in an *agriturismo* and the word is bringing back terrible memories. He pinches his eyes as if to indicate that either a) I should at least buy some gas if I am going to bother him with questions, or b) I have an accent, a hideous accent, and listening to me is painful for someone who loves the Italian language as he does. He shrugs, shakes his head. *"No,"* he says, *"non ci sono qui."*

"Any in this general area?"

"No."

"Can you recommend a good place for my family and me to stay?"

"No." He shakes his head and looks away, and I jog back across the road, sure he is wrong. He isn't the *agriturismo* type, or he's still furious about his ex-wife, or he hates Americans, or his dog was recently killed by a Kangoo driven by a foreigner.

We stop next at a deli, which, according to a sign on the front door, is closed. Pushed beyond my ordinary politeness by the motivating effects of hunger, exhaustion, and guilt, I try the door anyway. It opens. I step in and go hopefully and optimistically down the aisle toward the deli counter. Two women in the kitchen at the back squint at me with a mixture of apprehension and annoyance and, when I ask about lodging nearby, hand me a phone book. I look up "Agriturismo", find seven of them listed, copy down the addresses and phone numbers, and justified at last, almost triumphant, thank the women and go back outside.

Outside, I hear screaming coming from the Kangoo, but there is a phone booth nearby so I ignore the screaming, walk over to the phone and dial. The phone, it seems, is out of order. I try it a second time and it is still out of order. A woman appears, just leaving the hairdresser's shop next to the deli, neatly coiffed and happy. I show her the addresses on my pad of paper and ask her which of the *agriturismi* is closest. "Oh no, no, none of them," she says. "They're far on the other side of the city."

We drive on.

Within a few minutes we have become entangled in Lucca's rush hour traffic, a horrendous soup of belching Fiats, Volkswagens, trucks and buses that clogs the road encircling the beautiful city's brown brick wall. At this point my good wife isn't quite as sure as I am about the *agriturismo*. "I see some signs for hotels," she says, "over there, Rol." She points down a

side road, but I can't very easily cut across the two lanes of
stalled traffic to get to that road. Or I don't want to. The negativity has caught me now, blown me out of the pleasant valley I
usually inhabit, and up onto a craggy mountainside. An old
stubbornness is rising up. Somewhere in the depths of me I
believe that, purely by force of will, simply because the world is
a fair place, I will find something better than a mere *hotel*. No, a
hotel isn't good enough for me now, not good enough for my
suffering family. No. We will stay in an *agriturismo*, a gorgeous
stone villa set in verdant Italian countryside, with its own restaurant, the walls lined with bottles of wine, the table covered
with a home-cooked four-course meal, the beds large and
warm, with soft pillows and thick, clean quilts. God owes the
tired man on the mountainside at least that much.

This is how my mind sometimes works, I'm sorry to say.

But I haven't stayed happily married all these years by being
a completely stubborn ass. Another few stop-and-go blocks
and I relent, make a left, drive around on side streets looking
for the hotels Amanda claims to have seen. My mother is silent, which means that the arthritis in her neck has been acti-
vated by all these hours of riding, and that she has reached the
bottom of her bag of tricks and decided to let the girls com-
plain all they want. Alexandra says, six or eight times, "When
are we going to *be* there?"

"Soon. Any minute. We're having a little trouble finding the
right place, that's all."

Her sister yells, "UP! UP! UP! AGGH!"

We see a hotel, but it looks gritty and cheap and the road in
front is full of loud trucks. How would the kids sleep in a place
like that? What kind of re-introduction to Italy would it be for
us, for my mother?

Trying another route away from the clogged outskirts, rely-
ing not on the map now but on my vaunted intuition, I end up

driving down a road that looks vaguely familiar. Soon I realize why: it is the road we have just come in on. Amanda points this out to me. Pauses. Says she remembers seeing a hotel somewhere on this road. In a few minutes we do, in fact, drive by the hotel, which is tucked between the noisy road and a river, and does not look particularly promising. But to please my good wife I make a sharp right turn and circle around behind it on a driveway that runs between two stone buildings and is three inches wider than the mirror-wingspan of the Kangoo. I stop, turn off the engine, and look at Amanda. With a diplomacy born of decades of marriage and fed by her basic good nature, she suggests that I go in alone and check out the rooms. I agree to do that.

Inside, the clerk seems surprised to see me, an actual potential customer. When he recovers, he brings me upstairs to inspect the available rooms, which look comfortable enough, but they are on separate floors, up a narrow set of stairs, no elevator. They are plain as dirt. They are in no way a reward for the trials of the day. In no way do they match my vision. We will either have to leave our half-ton of supplies in the car— always a risky move in this part of the world—or carry them up three narrow flights, then load the girls back into the car and go out on the town in search of dinner. No. We drive back toward Lucca.

Just outside one of the arches in Lucca's Renaissance wall, there is a sign saying Absolutely No Parking. I park there, beneath the sign. It is actually very easy to park there. I just pull to the curb and punch the emergency flashers button on the Kangoo. I may punch it with more force than is necessary, but I punch it, open the door, and leave the keys in the ignition in the unlikely even somebody in authority cares about the illegal parking job. I look across the seat again at Amanda, hoping, I suppose, for forgiveness, understanding, a route down off the craggy slope, a good suggestion.

Amanda has her quirks, we have our differences, but she is the most even tempered of wives, a good person to have nearby in difficult moments. True, she will sometimes settle for a hotel when something finer is called for, and, true, she will sometimes assert with confidence statements of "fact" that should be tempered with doubt. But, at that particular moment I am not in any position to hold those things against her. "I remember this gate," she says, surely. "There's a tourist office just inside."

I volunteer to check it out. My mother volunteers to come with me. We step out of the Kangoo and go in through the portal. But there is no tourist information office here, except in Amanda's memory. For the fifth or sixth time that day, we ask directions. "Turn here," a kindly older man tells us. He is stooped and walking with a cane, and, from his tone, is obviously a lifelong resident of Lucca. "Go straight," he says, "*diritto*. You'll see it."

But we don't see it. I can feel, somewhere just on the far side of Lucca's forty-foot-thick brick wall, my children's patience burning like a fuse in the gathering darkness. After a futile, five-minute search along Lucca's cobbled streets, I approach a well-dressed elderly couple, and they, too, seem pleased to be of assistance. He, too, is walking with a cane; she has one arm hooked inside his. As though helping this polite young foreigner is the highlight of their evening *passegiata*, they direct us with an old-world dignity that cuts like the clean blade of conscience into the rough temper I've been working up. My mother and I thank them, then retrace our steps half a block and turn into the courtyard they've indicated—I am pretty sure I've understood them correctly—but there are no signs for a tourist information office in the courtyard.

We see a trio of uniformed policemen—*carabinieri*— walking toward one of the buildings. I jog over in their direction, and they turn, laconically, and look at me the way only a *carabinieri* can look at you, one finger on the trigger-guard of the submachine gun. The finger is intended to make you stop jogging as you approach. The look is intended to make you understand that *carabinieri* are highly trained and courageous servants of the people, paid to outwit drug traffickers, terrorists, and Euro-counterfeiters, but in no way obliged to give directions to tourists. They listen to my question with an off-putting wash of impatience and suspicion marking the tanned skin of their handsome faces. A pause, a desultory movement of one chin. At last, two words of direction.

The office, it turns out, is located where the *carabinieri* indicated it would be, hidden away in an alley, off a courtyard, through a door. Perfect kind of central location lost tourists can easily stumble upon. And it is closed. Has just closed, in fact, five minutes ago, so the workers there can have their dinner. Will not open again for another hour.

My mother and I walk out of the courtyard and down the street that leads back to the portal, stopping once at a travel agency where I persuade the woman clerk with polite, insistent, less-than-perfect Italian to call the nearest hotel for us. But when I get on line with the hotel reservations desk, it turns out that the rates are far beyond our budget—almost four hundred dollars for a night's sleep. And the bed situation isn't exactly right, the parking problematic. I put one fist in my pocket and squeeze it around the *agriturismo* idea. My mother and I walk back to the illegally parked Kangoo and three expectant faces.

We drive on.

Darkness falls. Out of local options now, so exhausted we are all past the point of complaining, we climb back onto the Autostrada in the direction of Florence. And then, acting on some mysterious impulse, I take the exit for Montecatini

Terme. "Terme" is either a short form of "the end" as in "the end of life" as in "terminal". Or it means "bath" in Italian, as in "thermal baths". I am thinking maybe I can find one of those baths and drive the Kangoo directly into it. I am driving like a true Italian—fuming, burnt out, needing sleep and food—but clinging nevertheless, with every ounce of my legendary stubbornness (which can be a good or a bad trait, depending on the circumstances), to my vision of a fine meal and an extraordinarily restful night.

We pull into the outskirts of the busy little city of Montecatini Terme—like lunch hour, rush hour is protracted in Italy, extending from four to eight. There, in the freckled urban darkness, we see what appears to be a miraculous apparition—a tourist information office, open at seven p.m. The only problem is that we have already passed it. So I do what any Italian would do: I make a U-turn across three lanes of oncoming traffic.

"Rol?" my mother squeaks from the back seat.

"What are you doing?" Amanda wants to know.

But I have full confidence in what I am doing. Hard on the heels of the risky U-turn, I swing the Kangoo into the parking area near the kiosk, and park, without consciously intending to, beside a car with a blue light on top. Two traffic policemen are standing beside the car and it is clear from their expressions that they have borne witness to my Italian-class U-turn. I'm not sure whether I am about to be arrested or applauded. I wish them *"Buona sera"*. They respond with twin small nods. I walk over to the booth. Two young men are on duty there, but no, it turns out to be some other kind of tourist information office, for some other kinds of tourists, and no, they do not know of any country inns in this general vicinity. They wave me in the direction of downtown and mumble the word *albergo*. Hotel.

Going back to the Kangoo, I stop to ask the traffic cops if

there might be an *agriturismo* in the area. "Ask at that booth," one of them says.

"I just did."

"And what? They couldn't help you?" The older of the two officers marches back to the booth with me—it's clear now that they have greatly admired my skill in making the illegal U-turn and are considering me for membership in the elite club of true Italian drivers—and have a few rough words with the boys. One of them manages to come up with the name of a hotel, but the directions are complicated. I ask the kind young fellow to repeat them, so as to be sure. He switches to English, or what might be English, and I can't understand him so I repeat the directions in Italian, which apparently humiliates him in front of his co-worker and the traffic cop. He glares and looks away. But by then I am beyond caring about the feelings of curt young men in Tourist Information booths. I walk back to the Kangoo. The other cop blows hard on his whistle, raises a hand, and holds up three lanes of cars so we can leave the parking lot and merge onto the main street without waiting, and I like to think this gesture is one of high esteem, in honor my illegal U-turn.

In quickly-moving traffic, half a mile closer to the center of town, we come to a fork in the road and can't be sure which way to turn. Did he say left here? Is this the light?

While we're pondering, the flow of traffic carries us to the right side, past the fork, and the question becomes moot. Three blocks further along it is clear to us that we should have gone left. We try to backtrack, get lost in a maze of dark, one-way streets, nothing open at that hour. Another block, and we pass two hotels.

"They have a guarded parking lot," Amanda notes.

"We won't have to unload all the luggage," I say hopefully. My grip has loosened on the *agriturismo* idea. Bludgeoned and battered, deprived of sleep, I am at last ready to surrender.

I slow down so Amanda can read the sign on the first hotel's front door: Closed for the Season.

Second hotel, same news.

At last, after a few more blocks, we come upon an open hotel, with a high metal fence around the parking lot. But, inside, at the last minute, the clerk tells me that the restaurant, *sfortunatamente*, is closed at this time of year. He looks at me expectantly. I reach for my wallet. In one final, desperate effort, a crazy, blind shot, I say: "I'd like to make it easy for my family to eat. Would there happen to be an *agriturismo* close by?"

He admits that there is one, fairly close by, and volunteers to call the place and see if they have any rooms. He dials, asks a couple of questions, makes a reservation for two rooms, then hangs up and gives me careful directions.

"Did you ask how much it costs?" Amanda wants to know when I'm back in the car.

I do not answer.

We drive several miles along a dark, two-lane road and somehow miss the turn for the *agriturismo*. Standing in the hotel lobby, watching the clerk's lips as he spoke, thinking how generous he was to be giving me directions to a competing establishment, pondering the manifold verb tenses in his glorious language, afraid to ask how much the *agriturismo* would cost, knowing Amanda would want to know, I was certain I understood: left at the top of the hill; follow the road into another commercial area; look for signs. But we don't see any signs. "When are we going to *be there*?" Alexandra is asking. Juliana screams: "NO SEAT! NO SEAT!" In the parking lot of a dark strip mall, I get out and ask directions of two men who are, it seems clear to me, assessing a cache of stolen merchandise in the trunk of a car. The men shift their attention to the fully-packed Kangoo, run their eyes over me from shoes to shirt. I make my karate face, pull my tired shoulders straight. One of the men points us back a block. We climb a dark and desolate road into the hills, and over the din in the back seat my mother inquires, innocently, pleasantly, appearing to mean no criticism of her son's judgment, as only a mother can: "Who would believe there'd be a hotel here?"

But at the end of the dark road we see the sign: *Amici del Colle*. Friends of the Hill. *AGRITURISMO*. We decide that we are friends of the hill. And then we drive down a side road onto the grounds of a gorgeous mirage. Beautiful three-story stone villa, tall windows, balconies, tile roof, large swimming pool, the lights of Montecatini Terme twinkling below in a bowl of hills.

The rooms have luxurious tiled Jacuzzis, TVs, and comfortable beds. The restaurant is right downstairs. We are the only guests. We bring up a few necessary bags and settle ourselves in for this meal: *farro*, the hearty bean and bulgur soup you find mainly near the Ligurian coast. Then an excellent *penne*, cooked just right; a mixed grill of rabbit, beef, and pork, two glasses of the good house red wine for me, a fresh salad, cheesecake and tiramisu, coffee for my mother. We talk a bit with Thomas, the handsome, likeable son of the owner of the place. He tells us that his father is a famous Italian boot designer, and shows us a pair of boots in a display case there: knee-high, bright red leather with white eyelets and spike heels. I ask Amanda, whose taste in clothes runs to the exceptionally modest, if she would like a pair for her next birthday. She smirks.

We go upstairs and sleep the sleep of the dead. Early the next morning, after a breakfast of cappuccino, bread and jam, and a little more conversation with Thomas, we wander the manicured grounds of *Amici del Colle,* gazing up at the terraces of olive trees and grapevines, then down at the interwoven hills. "I could live here," my mother says. The girls run about shrieking in the sun. Amanda takes some photos, I repack the car. "I could live here," my mother says again, as we're driving away. Alexandra sings out, "Italy is great!" and her sister chimes in, "Yah! Yah!"

In retrospect I can say this: If we knew on that morning what we would soon discover, we would have called and cancelled the Contigliano reservations, lost the deposit, and spent the entire vacation at Friends of the Hill. But alas, sorry to say, *sfortunatamente*, we did not do that.

<u>8</u>

In a glorious mood, sated and rested, we leave *Amici del Colle*, wind our way out of Montecatini Terme, and locate the Autostrada without incident. Now, at last, we are heading for our home in the hills, and all of us are optimistic. A good meal and a good night's sleep can do that for you. Though a few wisps of jet-lag remain, I am thinking clearly and driving brilliantly and I know then that the Contigliano house will be a wonderful place—soothing to the nerves and the spirit, refreshing to skin and bones that have suffered through such a bitter couple of months. Thoughts of that cold Massachusetts air remind me, after we've been on the Autostrada for a while, that the owner of the house had suggested I call the neighbors before we arrive and ask them to turn up the heat and generally make sure the house is ready. So we pull off the Autostrada into a rest area, and, in the convenience store there, after a few minutes of frustration and some helpful hints from the clerk, I figure out how to work the phone card. It's a smart system, useful in those pre-cell-phone days: you pay a certain amount for the card and then insert it in a slot in the top of the pay phone console. There's a small screen on which the amount of your credit appears, and then, once you place the call, you see the number of minutes remaining before you have to top off the card again.

The call I place is to our future neighbor, a woman named

Agnese. She answers, as Italians do, not by saying "Hello" but by saying "*Pronto!*" which means "ready." I respond with *buon giorno,* and tell her who I am. Orlando, the American. She's happy to hear from me. She's been expecting us. *"La casa e' preparata?"* I ask. Is the house prepared? *"O, si, si. Preparata. Si."*

That accomplished, my faith in our good fortune buttressed by the small victory with the phone card, the triumph of communicating in Italian via telephone, the important piece of good news—*la casa e' preparata*—and, mainly, the morning coffee from *Amici del Colle,* I return to the car, and drive out of the parking area with *confidenza.* Soon we merge onto A-1, the main Interstate that traces the spine of the Apennines from Milan to Naples. In the mountains of north-central Italy, A-1 is only two lanes wide in each direction. The right lane of the southbound side is thick with trucks carrying goods south from the factories of Milan and Torino and Dusseldorf and Amsterdam. And the left lane is a kind of testosterone-infused daredevil proving-ground for the great driving machines of western Europe. Running on a solid night's sleep, and the coffee, and the optimism, with a happy wife studying the map and guidebook, and two happy kids and a happy mother playing word games in the back seat ("I've found another homonym, Dad," Alexandra announces, "You" and "U" the letter!") I am a match for anyone—anyone!—on that road. If only the car were a BMW or a Mercedes, if only I didn't have to consider the well being of my loved ones!

I chug along at 120 Km/hr in our decidedly domesticated Kangoo, sliding into the right lane for a moment between grumbling eighteen-wheelers, but only long enough to let some bachelor in a Porsche fly past, then taking the big lane again, the man's lane, swooping down past Florence and into the *bel paese's* mountainous heart. My thoughts go like this: Another day or so and we'll be settled in to our mountain retreat, the kids playing in the yard, Amanda wandering the grounds with her camera, my mother reading, or practicing sand wedge shots out back.

We pass Incisa, Valdarno, Terranuova, and roll through the pretty high hills around Arezzo, not far from Michelangelo's place of birth. The air in those hills—they rise to almost 2,000 feet—is disconcertingly cold. An aberration, I tell myself, a twenty-four-hour dip caused by some rogue cold front rushing through. Italy is warm. Italy is the home of my soul.

Not far from Perugia, we trade the Autostrada for a smaller, less busy, two-lane road and hurtle along, hungry again, looking for a place to have lunch. It is amazing how hungry one gets in Italy. I'm not sure how that works, exactly; after all, we have been just sitting here in our leased Renault, burning more gas than calories, doing nothing to work up an appetite. Maybe it's the air. Maybe it's the memory of past meals, awakened in the folds of the mind like sleeping children, excitable, happy children who, once stirred, go running about in every room of the house, making noise.

Once, in Torino, on our first, very brief visit to Italy (we stayed less than a day), Amanda and I stopped in an eight-table lunch place near the old center of that city and ate a dish of pasta with tomato sauce and a salad, bread, wine, coffee. There was nothing fancy about that food, no special ingredients like truffles, pork cheek, or goose breast—no elaborate presentation. But it was a perfect meal, everything fresh, everything cooked and seasoned exactly right, and the simple perfection of it stays with us still, fifteen years later. Another time, a friend took us to a hole-in-the-wall place in Rome called der Pallaro, where there was no menu, only a steady stream of small portions coming out of the kitchen: boiled artichoke, pasta in a meaty red sauce, a small cut of succulent pork, white beans in oil, sliced pears in sauce, sweet *panna cotta* or cooked cream, some gorgonzola cheese, a liqueur.

From time to time, as we speed southward, that memory, or one very much like it, sticks an elbow into its neighboring gray matter. Pulling out from behind a tractor trailer with Austrian plates, I think of a glass of white wine I'd had from an unlabeled bottle in a Sardinian restaurant, also in Rome. Watching a Lancia fly up close to our rear bumper, with the trucks roaring along in tight formation in the right lane making it impossible to move aside, I am reminded of a dish of spaghetti in Santa Margherita Ligure, with a dollop of creamy, garlicky pesto made from just-picked basil, lying in a pool on top. The hot, soft insides of sugary crescent rolls in Abruzzo; the half-dollar-sized octopus glistening in olive oil at the side of a plate of ziti in Lucca; the field mushrooms, the rabi, even that heated ham and cheese panini in a bar in Tuscany; thick soups, creamy desserts; a place in Venice that served salads of carrots and greens so fresh they seemed to be growing as you ate them, a chicken *a la parmigiana* in Trento. Maybe it's just the monotony of the road. Maybe the word "Italy" itself, those three syllables, stimulates some acupuncture meridian that has to do with digestion. I don't know. I know only that, when we draw close to Perugia, we're hungry again.

Not far from the very beautiful, if not very clean-looking, Lago Trasimeno—Hannibal routed the Romans on those shores—we see, near the city of Castiglione del Lago, the first in a series of crossed fork and spoon signs that always set the saliva glands to working, no matter what language you dream in. We follow those signs, one after the next, and they lead us into a dead-end park on the steel-blue lake. There are actually not one, but two restaurants in this dead-end park on the lake. One of them is closed, and the other . . . also closed. Set to open, a sign on the door states, the following day.

Next, we follow a different set of fork-and-spoon signs,

moving back toward the highway this time, and find a place that's open and that has the advantage of a parking lot where we can keep an eye on the overpacked Kangoo. It has the additional advantage, my scouts tell me once we're inside, of toilets with seats on them. At this establishment, which shall remain unnamed, we have a disappointing lunch—spaghetti with pesto, and, for me, a watery glass of white wine. Afterwards, as we pay the bill, we talk a bit with a wide-faced fellow who sits by the cash register and ogles my two young girls in a way that makes my fists tingle. Maybe I'm wrong, though it's not as if I have this feeling often. But something is amiss about this guy. There's something obscene in his smile, some squalid aura hanging around him, spelled out clearly in the movement of his eyes. On the wall opposite the cash register he has hung a picture of himself with a 25-pound bass he'd caught in the dirty lake, and even that innocent portrait seems to me to speak of some polluted self-absorption. "So how is it there in America?" he wants to know. "The people rich?'

"Some of them," I say, and I usher the girls out the door into the unseasonably cold air.

By late afternoon we are closing in on Contigliano, passing through the city of Terni, which, before it was severely damaged by World War II Allied bombing raids, must have been an attractive place. It's an industrial center now—as then—and the birthplace of St. Valentine. We pass flat-roofed factories chugging out smoke, and blocks of pastel-colored apartment houses with not very much to recommend them. There are snow topped mountains in the near eastern distance. The air is cold enough to make us think we've been driving north the past two days instead of south. We get lost only briefly in Terni, however, following the signs of course, then leave the city on a switchback road, driving past solitary souls hunting for mushrooms or truffles in high, cold fields.

In her lap, Amanda holds the printed-out email directions to our home in the hills. We curve and dip and raise a trail of dust through the hamlet of Greccio, with its hillside chapels built in memory of Saint Francis of Assisi (I promise my mother we shall visit them, a promise I will never keep). We all cheer when we see the first sign for Contigliano, only a few kilometers away now. There are more winding, dusty roads, nice views of mountains and forests to either side. Twelve kilometers, eight kilometers. Big wave of optimism and expectation swelling up around us.

But when we at last pull into the town of Contigliano itself, there is not much cheering to be heard. Not that there is anything particularly wrong with Contigliano. It is, in fact, a perfectly pleasant Italian town, with the gray stone buildings of the historical section high on a rise, old men on benches waiting for the bus to Rieti, and one or two teenagers shuffling along in sloppy pants, headphones pinching mops of hair. But compared to our dreams, my dreams at least . . .

And we are looking for food. In a past life, perhaps a long past life, Amanda was certainly a quartermaster in the treks of Marco Polo, and she is a magician when it comes to setting up a working kitchen in unlikely places, stocking the shelves, finding bargains. When we lived in the Soviet Union, working for the U.S. Government there on traveling cultural exhibitions, she made pancakes with bacon and real maple syrup—on a hot plate in our hotel rooms no less—and hosted a regular rotation of our food-deprived co-workers, desperate for an American breakfast. Now, sensibly enough, she wants to pick up a few things in downtown Contigliano so we can have breakfast in our rented house the next morning—sitting out on the patio, steaming cups of coffee in our hands, bread toasting in the kitchen, the mountains shining in the distance, green twists of fairway outlined there among wisps of fog on the plain. The directions in her lap inform us that there is a Co-Op market in the center of Contigliano. We find it without much trouble at all. It is closed. The butcher shop is also closed. The bakery. The pharmacy. When we ask one of the town's elderly pedestrians the reason for this, we are told that it is Thursday.

So we stop in the center of Contigliano for hot chocolate, coffee, and fresh-squeezed juice and cannoli and cookies and croissants in a combination bar/*pasticceria*, then drive out of town in the fading cold light, following our landlady's directions. Left at the bus shelter two miles from town. Climb. Soon we pass a tiny stone church—exactly where it is supposed to be according to our map—with darkening fields and a few houses to either side. The dirt and gravel road grows steeper there, steep, very narrow, and so serpentine that, above one turn, there is a mirror posted on a pole so you can see around the corner and perhaps avoid a head-on crash. Soon the road becomes a track, barely wide enough for the Kangoo's wheels. But this is part of the charm, is it not? Up and up, small stones spitting beneath the tires. Now, in the last of the light, in the last moments of unblemished optimism, we come upon Agnese's house. For a second or two it seems as though the road will pass straight through her back yard; then it does. We see pigs, ducks, chickens, rabbits, goats. The road dissolves into an undefined dirt track, and there is suddenly a pack of large, possibly friendly mongrels scrambling around the front tires. We stop. Agnese comes over and welcomes us, a sturdily-built, dark-haired, gentle-spirited woman with calloused hands. Mimmo, the sixty-five-year-old caretaker, comes over, too, his craggy face holding up a pair of thick round eyeglasses with black frames. We make introductions all around. They point to a small house farther up the hill and say they will come help us move in. "*Bene'*," we say. "*Va bene'. Grazie.*"

Attempting to make a strong first impression, I accidentally stall the Kangoo three times on the hay-strewn rocky road. Three times I let the clutch out and push on the gas and feel that ugly jolt, then silence. Mimmo and Agnese watch us, the dogs prance around. I start it up again, push on the gas more firmly, ease out the clutch. Clunk. Silence. Out of the corner of my eye I see Mimmo turn away in disgust. Agnese folds her hands in front of her. I make a sound that is meant to be a self-deprecating laugh. I try again. The dogs are leaping up on the sides of the Kangoo now because it is apparent even to them that the alien vehicle will remain stationary; soon they will lift a leg and mark the tires as their own. But I get it going at last, the dogs dart out of the way into the mountain darkness, and we scoot up the last hundred yards to our perfect vacation home.

Mimmo arrives promptly, driving a green, rusting, dented, three-wheeled utility truck with rakes and other tools clanging around in the back. He opens the house for us. It really is an attractive house—stucco, one-story, with a small porch out front and a tile roof . . . and it is as cold as an igloo. The floors are tile, the walls stone, lined with bookcases filled with wonderful books in several languages. Everything just as we'd imagined—only we'd imagined it thirty degrees warmer. Three bedrooms, kitchen, one long living room with comfortable couches—just as we'd been promised. Except colder.

"Mimmo," I want to say, but my throat has been closed by a small tornado of anger. "I called and asked if the house was prepared, and Agnese said it was. I have two little kids and my mother here, and it's forty god-damned degrees in the bedrooms." But behind his thick spectacles Mimmo presents a dour manner and, on this first meeting at least, doesn't seem particularly overjoyed to have the American family here, about to move in and complicate his life. He speaks not a word of English. And I cannot trust my Italian at this moment, and I want to cultivate a friendly relationship, be a good citizen of the world. And I am too angry to speak. As we are going out the front door together, with the dogs prancing around and the girls exploring, Mimmo asks, in what seems to me a disdainful tone: "Why didn't you park on the lawn?"

A spurt of anger escapes. I try, in my imperfect Italian, to say: "Because, in America, Mimmo, we don't just casually park on the lawns of people we don't know. We have great respect for lawns."

He shrugs. He leads me down and around the side of the house to a basement door and, once we are inside, shows me how to turn on the heat, this gauge this way, that gauge that way. I am good with my hands, a very good carpenter in fact, but gauges give me trouble, and I can never seem to remember directions like these at first—even in English—unless they're written down. Mimmo mumbles when he speaks, and I have to ask him to repeat everything, so that he now thinks I'm an incompetent American who can't drive a stick-shift up a hill and who doesn't understand a simple set of gauges that must be turned this way first, then the lever, here, you see, on the furnace, but not too much or it will explode, and then this gauge, just here, see, then the gas goes on, the water . . .

Why, I want to say, couldn't you have done this yesterday? But by this point I am frozen, to choose a bad word, in an evil memory. Fifteen or eighteen years earlier, when Amanda and I had been working in the USSR for thirteen straight months, and were about to leave for home, stopping for a European vacation on route, we saw an advertisement tacked up on a bulletin board at the American Embassy in Moscow. The title of the ad was—I will never forget this—"Chateau in the South of France." We had some money then, having saved our hardship pay and some of our per diem. We called the number on the ad. The owner of the chateau turned out to be a French woman who shall remain unnamed, wife of an American journalist working the Moscow bureau, and she sounded friendly and trustworthy. The house, she said, had a view of the ocean, there was a swimming pool and tennis courts nearby, a cozy patio in the yard.

Imagine the fantasies we concocted around this chateau! Imagine what it's like to have worked for a year in provincial communist backwaters like Rostov-na-Donu and Irkutsk, places with mud streets and Lenin museums, places where, for most of the year, you couldn't get so much as a salad or a glass of orange juice or a decent cut of meat, or on some nights a hot bath or shower. And then, when this year is over and you are bound for the luxuries of Western Europe, imagine that you see a sign saying, "Chateau in the South of France". Imagine that the rent is surprisingly reasonable.

We flew from Moscow to Frankfurt, rented a car there, and made our way south through the Black Forest and down toward the French Riviera with dreams of this magnificent chateau performing a sort of ballet in our minds. We had another complicated set of directions, which we dutifully followed, but there was no house, no chateau, where we expected it to be. We retraced our steps and tried again, up the road, left, right. Strange, we were in a trailer park, second time now. Very strange. There must have been some mistake, some miscommunication having to do with the various languages involved. We retreated to the nearest town, called the caretaker, who came to meet us and led us back up the road and . . . to a trailer in the trailer park. The community swimming pool was closed and scum-coated. The nets on the tennis court were sagging. There was, in fact, a view of the ocean—a blue speck thirty miles in the distance.

The caretaker was kind and well meaning—he hadn't written the ad, after all—and, with his thin, strong build and craggy, dark-haired looks, might have been Mimmo's karmic cousin. He unlocked the door of the trailer and we followed him in. He was showing me how to turn on the gas that heated the hot water for the place, for its sink and tiny shower. I remember this as if it were yesterday. I am standing close beside him, listening to a language I studied in graduate school, more than a decade earlier. I am looking at gauges, levers, and switches below the kitchen sink, trying to listen carefully through a fog of pure fury. I do not speak a word to him. I cannot speak a word. Amanda thanks him, he leaves. We sleep in the trailer one night, then take an apartment in Bandol for the week, and the Frenchwoman refuses to give us a refund.

So, as Mimmo, in his relentless, mumbled Italian, is showing me how to turn the dials to heat the house in which my children and my mother are now shivering, I am having a flashback to the Chateau in the South of France. Very unfair of me, because, unlike the Chateau, this house is just as it had been described to us. Except colder. The sun has long ago gone down. The temperature outside is sinking toward the freezing mark. In Italy.

Upstairs again, Mimmo and I try to figure out how to turn the gas on in the kitchen, then, with less success, how to work the oven. The oven, apparently, is considered female terrain, and, as we fail there repeatedly, Mimmo pronounces the first of several phrases by which I will forever remember him: "About this I know exactly nothing." Together, we try to figure out how to take the little plastic cover off the thermostat in the living room, but Mimmo doesn't know much about this either. When he leaves, I go outside with the intention of catching a solitary breath of air and turning the Kangoo around so it will be easier to unpack. And I do, in fact, turn it around without incident. But then I try to back it up the steep, slick incline of the lawn and it stalls. I try again. It stalls a second time. No one is watching. Hearing the familiar *thunk*, the dogs from down below race up and circle the car excitedly. Finally, I put the emergency brake on, rev the engine, blast the horn to chase the dogs out of the way, and then take the brake off and race backwards up the lawn in the Italian mountain blackness. I make it safely to the top of the rise, but when I turn off the engine there is a truly awful smell.

Burning clutch.

Sitting out there in the dark in the Kangoo, chilled, jet-lagged, with the dogs jumping up on the doors and the rest of the family inside wrapped in blankets, I picture myself calling Valter the next day and telling him I have burned out the clutch on our new Renault, and Valter asking me how that happened, and me telling him the truth, and Valter telling me, kindly, that there is a clause in the contract about burnt clutches, and that we are now required to drive to the nearest certified Renault dealer, which is all the way back in Milano, and have the clutch repaired, and pay for it out of our own pockets.

I step out of the car into a breaking wave of pessimistic feelings, climb up onto the deck, and manage, with awkward exertions of my shins and boots, to keep the dogs from getting into the house. Inside, we have a small emergency: no one can figure out how to work the VCR. (This is a bit more important to us than it might be to another family because Alexandra has a lung condition, cystic fibrosis, that required us, in those days, to do chest physical therapy for half an hour every evening, a nightly regimen that meant she had to sit and lie still in various positions while one of her parents drummed on her back, shoulders, and sides. This was much more tolerable for her when she was watching something entertaining on the screen. So one of the attractions of the house was the fact that there would be a VCR that worked with American movies.)

Behind the television (Italians call it the "Tee Voo") is a conglomeration of wires that rivals the gauges in the cellar for technical complexity. The wires lead here and there and are plugged, in a way that would not pass any electrical inspection that I know of, into a dangling compound outlet. There are two remotes. I spend twenty minutes fussing with the wires and the remotes, pushing various combinations of buttons, trying different channels, pulling out the email instructions and changing antennas, angles, positions. Getting nowhere. Amanda, who is upset and disappointed, but not as angry, takes a turn and gets it working, more or less, within a few minutes. Alexandra puts in her tape of *The Sound of Music*, but there is all kinds of trouble on the screen, none of it having to do with the von Trapp family and the Austrian Nazis. The tape whirs and wiggles, a spaghetti of white lines crisscrossing the picture. I fool around with the tracking button and solve this problem fairly well. But then, while I am sitting on the cold floor with my oldest daughter, drumming on the tops of her shoulders from behind, and while Amanda is making an inventory of the kitchen supplies and utensils, and while my mother is unpacking her bags and placing neatly folded sweaters into drawers, our nineteen-month-old Juliana wanders in a curious way around the large, tile-floored room for a few minutes then vomits all over her white wool sweater.

We clean her and wash her, finish up the chest PT and then drive back into Contigliano for a good sausage pizza at a friendly little place called The Garden. The owners—husband, wife, shy, teenage, English-speaking daughter—know something about hospitality, and, perhaps sensing that we have been in a chilly house, seat us by the fireplace. They tell us it has been an unusually cold winter, that (since we are Americans they must imagine this will be important to us) there is a McDonald's in Rieti, where they themselves eat only about once a year, and that the previous resident of our house had been a wonderful man, a *professore*, who'd died suddenly in his

63

sleep.

We enjoy the meal, pay them, thank them, drive back to the house, dress in thermal underwear, and crawl into our beds, wrapping ourselves tightly in the covers. For the time being, Amanda and I are not speaking to each other, a sour and temporary turn of events which happens occasionally when we travel—usually at a point in the first few days of a trip, when my imagined world is fading out and the real one fading in. This respectful if uncomfortable silence is broken when, in the middle of the night, Juliana throws up again, lying in her crib. Amanda and I work as a team: clean her, comfort her, change the bedclothes in the crib, lay a towel down. Another hour and she throws up a third time. We try to give her some water and she won't take it. She is dazed, feverish. Amanda holds her for a while, gets her to take a gulp or two of breast milk, and then puts her back into the crib and she makes it through the rest of the night in a fitful sleep, stirring occasionally and mumbling things indecipherable. I know this because I lie awake for most of that night, too, exhausted though I am, staring at the ceiling.

2

Next morning, the radiators seem to be working—a puff of warmth, the soft fragrance of burned dust—a good sign. In the mumbling confusion of the previous evening, my new friend Mimmo and I must have turned at least one of the dials in the right direction. When I throw open the tall wooden shutters of the main room, the sun comes streaming in through the east-facing windows, and the house is clearly a few degrees warmer than it had been the night before. Amanda and I are, as always, hoping for the best.

The view eastward toward Mount Terminillo is startling in the morning sun. Slanting down from our concrete front porch is a hillside dotted with a widely scattered stucco homes, all of them surrounded by cultivated plots, with the road to Contigliano marked by parallel lines of poplar trees, snaking away below. Beyond the road lies a fog-wreathed plain, ten miles across, and, with the high peaks, it might be, as Amanda suggests, a scene of Mt. Fuji or a postcard of Bali.

Since there is no food in the house, we drive into town for breakfast, find the bar/*pasticceria* we visited the night before and have the classic Italian morning meal: brioches of various sorts washed down by cappuccino, macchiato, hot chocolate, or caffe latte. Low fiber, high sugar. Enough caffeine to propel the fully-loaded Kangoo for a few hundred miles. The pleasant, white-aproned woman behind the counter makes us fresh-squeezed blood orange juice, served in tall, thin glasses, with lots of pulp, while men in topcoats, and a few women in high heeled boots, stand at the counter sipping espresso and talking. It is a typical Italian morning scene, except that the newspaper headlines are all about preparations for the impending war, and through the windows we can see rainbow-colored banners hanging from sills and balconies P-A-C-E. PEACE.

After breakfast, we decide to drive across the plain to Rieti. It promises to be a simple trip—from the front windows of our house we could see the two-lane, paved road—but somehow the signs we follow deposit us, not on the road to Rieti, but against a train track in a kind of dead-end Contigliano bottomland. We pull up beside the only person we come across, a long-haired postman on a motor scooter. He starts to give us directions, then stops, says, "Just follow me. It's easier that way." And, ponytail bouncing, back wheel kicking up dust, he leads us along dirt roads until we reach pavement, the girls laughing the whole way at the sight of a man with bouncing hair and a mailbag, riding a motor scooter through the dust.

We cross the plain in a happy mood. Like many Italian cities, Rieti consists of a cluttered and not particularly attractive ring of businesses and new apartment buildings set around an historic center that dates back more than five hundred years. The historic part is set up on a hill and pocked with church steeples, clock towers, and tiled roofs. We wiggle the Kangoo through the busy, narrow streets there, find a place to park on a steep hillside (I sniff the clutch, seems okay), change money in a bank, and step into a cathedral where Juliana's happy voice mingles with her sister's in echoes against the marble walls.

The day is sunny and might be called warm, at least by the standards of a Massachusetts February. It has been months since I've held a golf club, so I am itching to play, or, at least, to drive by and introduce myself at the course. At the bank where we changed our Traveler's Cheques into cash, I'd asked directions to what I am referring to here as the Artone Golf Club. The teller seemed puzzled. "*Artone*," he said. Hm. "*Artone*." He turned to his colleague at the next window and asked: "Is there a golf course around here? Someplace called *Artone*?" She didn't know. I began to feel a creeping premonition. The house was cold, Artone non-existent. Very bad.

But the first teller left his post and motioned for me to follow, something, it seems to me, that would never happen in an American bank, where the tellers would be all-business, and the secure area strictly off-limits. We went along a hallway around back, the teller knocked on an office door, and, without waiting for an answer, barged in on two men in a loan conference. "Is there a golf course around here?" he asked the bank official sitting behind the desk. Golfers themselves, perhaps, neither the official nor his client seemed to mind this intrusion. The client asserted that there was not one, but two golf courses nearby. Artone, and La Foresta. I got directions to Artone, we spent a happy few minutes in the church, and after a bit more turning and gliding and dodging of pedestrians, we made our way south out of Rieti. Just beyond the clutter of its outskirts, we turned onto an ancient highway called the Salaria, or "Salt Road" (so named because it was the route the Romans used to transport salt from the sea to the capital), that leads all the way to Rome.

At this point in our Italian vacation, everything is fine. We have cash in our pockets. Juliana seems to have recovered from her overnight flu. Everything is fine, except that there is no evidence of an actual golf course on or near the Salt Road. Well past the mileage marker where it should have been, according to the bank customer's directions, I pull the Kangoo off the Salaria into a village square, get out and approach a knot of tough-looking young guys lounging there in the sunlight.

Leather jackets, cigarettes, faces unbroken by a single smile, these *ragazzi* are either playing hooky, unemployed, or conspiring to commit a crime. But they are happy to be of assistance. They turn us back toward Rieti. "You'll see the sign," one of them says, from behind his dark glasses. "Can't miss it."

We do see the sign. Right side. The sign leads us down a road that bears some resemblance to the road that runs through Agnese's back yard, except that it is flat. Half a mile of this—the road narrowing and deteriorating—and we see the telltale small flags waving in the wind. My heart rises up. I know that my mother's heart rises up, too. "There it is, Ma," I say. Another hundred yards and we notice that the flags are planted on flat, featureless strips of brown and green grass that look like our yard on the day before I mow. The holes we can see from the road run back and forth beside each other in unimaginative patterns. The fairways are treeless and short. This, then, is the "challenging and picturesque nine-hole layout with the mountains rising into snow-capped peaks not far from the fairways and greens".

When I recover from the initial shock, I pull into a humble gravel parking lot and talk to a man about my own age who is taking clubs out of his trunk. "Is there another . . . longer . . . course nearby?"

"In La Foresta," he says.

"Is it . . . longer?"

"A bit longer. Hillier. About like this."

We thank him. We drive back toward Rieti, skirting the eastern edge of the city. We become not very badly lost, stop and asked directions only twice more. Hungry now, again, we climb a precipitous mountain road, the mood in the Kangoo having turned rather somber. "Golf course," I am saying between my teeth. "Challenging . . . Picturesque . . . Snow-capped mountains."

We come upon a restaurant overlooking the ski slope on Mount Terminillo, and we're seated in a large, sunlit room at a nicely set table. The restaurant is a notch fancier than our usual family lunch spots, the prices higher, but it will have to do because there are no other restaurants in the area, and because we don't want to drive all the way back into Rieti. *Spaghetti alle vongole*, is what I order, and when it arrives the clams are clinging to their small brown shells in a bath of oil, and the pasta cooked *al dente*. A glass of white wine. All is well. Everyone is happy again, nice view, mild day, a better golf course in the future.

But in the middle of the meal, Juliana throws up for the fourth time in less than twenty-four hours. We clean her, change her, and, worried now, finish our meal, then go out, with trimmed hopes, in search of golf course number two.

Not far from the restaurant, down another switchback road leading into a hidden valley, we find The Center of Italy Golf Course, and this one turns out to be more to our liking, a course with actual sand bunkers, regulation length holes, real putting greens. On our trips in those days, when Beetlebah was along, we worked a fair playing rotation—a little fairer to me, the true golf nut and occasional golf writer—but fair all the same. On this first day, my mother and I play and Alexandra comes along for the ride on the cart while Amanda takes Juliana for a sleep-inducing drive. My mother and Amanda will get the second shift on another day.

The Center of Italia Golf Course, *sfortunatamente*, does not accept credit cards, and the cart we rent does not have the power to carry us up the course's substantial hills. Since I am the only one comfortable driving on the steep stony paths, Alexandra and my mother have to get out and walk on the uphill grades to take weight off the feeble engine. But that doesn't matter too much: we are golfing, in Italy, the sun is out, and the course has some character. The last two holes are especially tough; I lose two balls in the pond that runs between them, but that doesn't matter either. My mother plays well and I am especially happy that Alexandra chose to come along for the ride because I harbor a secret hope that she and her sister will grow up to appreciate the complicated and often misunderstood joy that is golf. I won't force the sport on them, naturally. Gentle encouragement, some fun rides in the cart, the joy of hitting old balls into water hazards and laughing, then, slowly, some lessons, some visits to the driving range, some rounds on an easy course. Ten years down the road we'll all play together, a Merullo foursome. I envision it perfectly in my mind's eye. All is well.

When Amanda returns from the market, Juliana is asleep in her car seat in back. Alexandra greets her mother with a hug and says, "I should have gone with you and Ju Ju Bee, Mama."

10

At dinner that night, Juliana eats and drinks nothing. On the previous night she fell asleep without much trouble, and we were hoping against hope that the flu had run its course and she'd wake up fully recovered. But during the night she vomited twice more. At breakfast in the sunny, but still uncomfortably cool front room, she sits in her booster seat with dull eyes and no appetite. By this point, it has been twenty hours since she's taken anything beyond a few ounces of breast milk, and I can feel, swirling in the air around my ears, that particular species of fear-coated nervousness you feel when your child is ill. Amanda and I watch her every second, keep trying with the water, with ibuprofen. Alexandra and my mother are worried, too. The cold house, the vomiting—what kind of vacation is this turning out to be?

After several attempts, we succeed in giving Juliana a sip of water, a bit more milk. Fifteen minutes later she throws up. It makes me think of the time we took Alexandra to Rome, three years earlier. She, too, woke up and vomited on the first day in our apartment there. She, too, refused food and water until we finally had to take her to a doctor, a good, English-speaking doctor, who ended up trying various remedies over the course of our three-hour visit and then pedaled off on his bicycle, in the rain, for suppositories.

But this time the situation seems worse; it has gone on

longer, and Juliana looks dangerously gaunt. By nine o'clock—Saturday morning now—I am crouching beside the telephone with the Rome directory open in front of me on the sofa, dialing the doctor who'd helped Alexandra. He is in Rome, true, an hour and a half away, but at least we know him, know he is good, and that he speaks English. No answer. I dial Molly's house—the woman from whom we rented the Rome apartment. No answer there either. I dial a famous children's hospital we'd driven by almost daily during our Rome vacation, and the nurse who eventually takes the call tells me it sounds serious. Juliana should be brought into the emergency room.

"We're in Contigliano," I say. "Near Rieti. Isn't there a hospital in Rieti?"

"Better to bring her here," she says, avoiding a direct answer but sending a message nonetheless. "All the doctors here speak English."

So we wrap up our sick child in a warm blanket and get back in the Kangoo. A cold drizzle is leaking out of the sky, obscuring our spectacular view and making the road down through Agnese's property as slick as oil-coated asphalt. In the back seat, Juliana is quiet, staring down at her arms and barely blinking. We stop for a hasty snack at our bar in Contigliano, with Juliana clamoring for water we can't give her because we worry it will just make her throw up again, then we cross the plain, cut through the outskirts of Rieti, follow the signs for the Salaria, somehow miss it, make an illegal U-turn, find the Salaria on the third try (by which point the children have heard some words young children should not hear) and head south, past the challenging and picturesque golf course we discovered the day before.

"We don't even have a map of Rome," Amanda says, at one point, but I wave that particular concern away. What map? Why do we need a map? We lived there for a month, drove every parish of the city and walked the rest. We'll find the hospital by memory, by instinct.

Ah, pride.

With the weekend traffic, and the rain, and a five-mile tie-up on the two-lane Salaria (because a work crew has decided to prune branches from the eucalyptus trees during the Saturday morning exodus from the capital) it is a two-hour drive to the outskirts of Rome. The hilly countryside is dotted with villas and gardens, and, even in its stripped-down, mid-winter state, has a somewhat soothing feel to it: people have lived here for thousands of years; families have survived all sorts of troubles. A little of that historical perspective rubs off on us—not much.

As we at last merge into the savagery of the city's Ring Road and start looking at the names of the exits there, I wish we had a map, but don't say so. We take what I believe to be the correct exit, splashing down into the frenzy, the craziness, the madness of Roman traffic, then we zigzag back and forth for a kilometer or two before surrendering and stopping in a gas station to ask for help.

"*Scusi*," I say, in my most careful Italian, to one of the attendants lounging in a doorless outbuilding. "We are trying to get to the hospital called Bambin' Gesu. My daughter is not well."

At the sound of the name of the hospital, the attendant makes a face. Eyes closed, eyebrows up, lips turned down. Dramatic pause. "Listen," he says, *Ascolta*, "it's just so complicated to give you directions to Bambin' Gesu that I will tell you only this: See that traffic light up ahead?" He stands, walks a few steps toward the Kangoo, and points down a street that is mobbed with cars, trucks, and *motorini* going, it seems, in five different directions at once. "See it? Go right at that light and then *sempre diritto*, understand? Always straight. Straight, straight. Eventually, you'll see a sign for the Metro. Stop there

73

and ask."

Under the best of circumstances, driving in Rome is a mad circus of vehicular absurdity. When you're trying to get a sick child to the hospital, it is a kind of inner circle of hell. Double-parking is considered one of the side-show acts, and this narrows the streets down to one lane, sometimes a lane and a half. Cars travel along these one and a half lanes three abreast, allowing a little room for the *motorini* to squeeze in and out between and around them. Trucks cut you off without the smallest compunction. From the side streets, drivers push the dented noses of their vehicles out into traffic aggressively, because if they are not aggressive they will be stuck there, in that side street, until the next Pope is chosen. If you hesitate for an instant—out of politeness, or caution, or because your wife takes three seconds to read the directions or you take three seconds to comprehend them—then something, a car, a truck, a scooter, will zip across just in front of your headlights from one side, the other, or both. You can not be a kind person behind the wheel of a car in Rome; you cannot be considerate. You must turn yourself into a warrior.

It is a circus, a madness, a blight on one of the great cities of the world. And with Juliana suffering in the back seat, we lose ourselves in that circus for the better part of a rainy hour. Over the course of that hour, we ask directions another four times. Our Italian is improving with each encounter: we almost understand most of the answers now, some of the time. He said left and go over something, but what was the something? A train trestle? A set of tracks? These are words we do not know, key words. Amanda and I occasionally argue in tense situations like this; please, show me the married couple that does not and let them come and give us lessons. I am stubborn, proud, worried sick. She thinks she recognizes landmarks, and that recognizing them will magically get us closer to

Bambin' Gesu, where the doctors will all speak English. She says things like, "There's the park we used to live next to." And I answer: "And tell me, what good, in God's name, is that going to do us now?"

At last, three hours after setting out on our hour-and-a-half drive into the city, we arrive at Bambin' Gesu, locate the emergency entrance, see a space in the parking lot that perches just up the treacherous winding street from that entrance. We pack Juliana into the stroller and put blankets over her, one of us has a tight grip on Alexandra's hand. We wheel our sick girl down the sidewalkless, shoulderless, curving street, cars zooming by an arm's length to our right. We go past an officious guard, through a wide set of doors, and into the emergency room. Now the ordeal will end, surely it will end: a competent, English-speaking doctor will see her, prescribe a medication; we'll regain our more or less healthy balance, go out and have a nice meal, watch the color and smile return to Juliana's face and the calm mutual understanding return to our marriage.

That is the dream. This is the reality: there are thirty other sick children in the waiting area of the emergency room. Fifty parents in various states of anxious exhaustion. The kids are coughing, screaming, wailing, crying, sneezing, sitting dazed and silent. Not a doctor to be seen. Not a nurse. Not a uniformed, official-looking person of any kind. Nearby is a hallway, with what appears to be examination-room doors leading off of it. Just as I am about to go down that hallway and find someone to ask, a kind woman with a sick child of her own tells us that a hospital employee will appear shortly, and that we should make our presence known to that person, and then we'll be seen according to a kind of triage system: sickest kids first.

A thin, blond woman in a nurse's uniform soon emerges from one of the rooms. We tell her we've driven all the way down from Rieti, which makes absolutely no impression on her. We say that our daughter hasn't eaten or drunk anything in twenty-four hours, that she's been throwing up all that time. The nurse takes down this information and tells us it will be a forty-minute wait. It is 12:30 p.m.

Amanda volunteers to take the first shift with Juliana, and I volunteer to take my mother and Alexandra out for a quick lunch. We cross the treacherous road, holding hands. We descend a very long set of stone steps into the old, once-working-class-now-fancified part of town called Trastevere, go into the first restaurant we see, and ask for the no-smoking section. The host sneers and leads us to our seats. We eat most of an unremarkable dish of pasta; my mother has coffee, I have a glass of wine, then I leave them to their dessert and hurry back up the steps to see what has happened. It is 1:45. Amanda has not moved. She tells me that three children have been seen so far. I take Juliana out of her arms so she can go get something to eat, and I wait. And wait. At last, at 2:40, our name is called over the loudspeaker and I carry Juliana down the hallway into one of the examination rooms. There, we are seen by a female doctor, fortyish, who speaks not a word of English. Not "Hello". Not "okay". Not anything. But the room is immaculately clean and modern, computers beeping away, and the doctor seems warm and efficient and smart. I tell her that, with the exception of a little water and breast milk, Juliana hasn't eaten or drunk anything for forty hours. The doctor draws some blood, checks this and that, tells me there is a bad flu going around the city, gives me some orange-flavored electrolyte solution for Juliana to drink, then tells me to go back to the reception area and wait. If Juliana drinks the solution and doesn't throw up, we can leave. If she throws up again, she might have to be admitted. "How long do you think it will be before we know?" I ask.

"Un ora, piu o meno." An hour, more or less.

While we were in the examination room, Amanda returned

from lunch, leaving my mother and Alexandra in the germ-free air outside. It is now five minutes to three. "We'll have to wait here an hour or so," I say, and she takes Juliana onto her lap and finds a seat in the crowded waiting room. My mother, Alexandra, and I go across the treacherous road and up to the Janiculum Hill, where Garibaldi and his men defended the city from attacking French troops in 1849. There, we watch a show of two hand puppets hitting each other violently over the head with bats and yelling at each other until one of them lets out a spectacular scream and collapses on stage. This is a children's show. When it is over, a man comes around with a hat, collecting Euros. Puzzled and upset by the puppet show, worried about her sister, Alexandra's mood is atypically restrained. We try to cheer her up by giving her a ride on the merry-go-round and a candy bar. Beetlebah and I get a view down over the beautiful city, all reds, browns and ochres, gilded domes and tiled rooftops, the towers of half-century-old cathedrals standing above an earth-toned wash of history. At four-thirty we return to the emergency room.

Amanda hasn't moved. I take over. I'm beginning to get to know the other people in the room, especially an interesting couple next to us. The man is six-three or six-four and the woman under five feet. His mother is there, too, toothless and serene and bearing a striking resemblance to her very tall son. Their child is at least as sick as Juliana. Next to them sits a wealthy-looking pair, the woman in leather jacket and jewels, holding a gorgeous seven or eight-year-old girl with long blond hair and large green eyes, dulled by illness. The father is short, muscular, angry, walking around with his fists clenched as if he wants to be out playing golf, or making deals, or, like me, he is simply unable to be still and calm when one of the loves of his life is suffering. At five-thirty the doctor sees us again. I say, "She wouldn't drink any of this."

And the doctor says, "Why not? It's orange-flavored."

"Because she's as stubborn as her father," I almost answer. Or, "Because she's figured out that when she puts anything into her mouth it makes her throw up, and she's decided she doesn't want to throw up any more." But the doctor—who has been seeing sick children for the whole long day—is calm, warm-hearted, and attentive, and she's done a bunch of tests, and she looks at Juliana as if it is her niece there, feverish and miserable on the table, and I like her. She tells me the blood tests were all fine. A stomach flu and nothing more. It will soon pass. She writes out two prescriptions and tells us we can leave, and when I ask her what we owe for our six hours there, our three consultations with her, our computerized blood tests, she says, "Nothing. You owe nothing."

Out the door we go into the rainy Roman evening, across the treacherous road, floating along in a mix of lingering anxiety and hope, all of us together now, surrounding the sick one, buoying her up. The fellow who takes payment for the parking lot has abandoned ship at this late hour, so that, too, turns out to be free. We leave the lot, fill the prescriptions at a *farmacia* where the attendants are white-coated and very serious about their work, and where you have to push a button on the exterior wall in order to be admitted. The medicine is not free.

To comfort ourselves after what might be described as a moderately stressful day, we decide we will have a meal in one of our favorite Roman restaurants, a place mentioned in passing here already a couple of times. This place (which no longer exists) is called Il Sardo al Angolo in Trastevere, and specializes in Sardinian food. I have the small magazine assignment to write about two golf courses in Rome, so maybe we'll spend the night and I can do that work on the following day and we can go to Sunday Mass in one of the city's great churches. Maybe we can turn a disaster into an adventure. Maybe everything will soon be fine.

We step through the door and see Angelo, the diminutive, mustachioed, white-haired waiter at Il Sardo, who recognizes us immediately though he's no doubt served a thousand or ten thousand customers since the last time we saw him. Angelo stands close by the table and chats for a while, moustache drooping, eyes sparkling, short thick fingers gently pinching Alexandra's cheeks and resting on Amanda's shoulder. "The little one is feeling not so good," he says, touching the side of Juliana's arm. "Not so very good." After our last visit, Amanda had sent him a photo she'd taken in this room, and he remembers it, thanks her for it, two years later.

As is his style, Angelo takes our order without writing anything down, then brings us the wonderful unleavened Sardinian bread and clean-tasting white wine we'd had here on more than one occasion during our Rome visit. In a few minutes my mother is served a lasagna she describes as, "soft as silk. Delicious. The best yet." I have a succulent roast piglet and a salad. Amanda goes with the eggplant parmesan. Alexandra likes the pasta. For the girl who is feeling not so good, the kind people at Il Sardo cook up a dish of plain rice (*senza niente* "without nothing" is the way you say it in Italian) but Juliana sits in a sorrowful curl in her mother's lap, refusing all food and drink.

Food heals. Nowhere is that more true than in Italy. I keep hoping to see Juliana accept one spoonful of rice, but she is buried in her illness, walled off from us. Still, the meal makes us hopeful—she's taking medicine now. It's a stomach flu. Whoever heard of a stomach flu lasting longer than a few days?

Arriverderci means "until we see each other again." After the meal and another short chat, we say that to Angelo and step back out into the drizzly Trastevere night, still checking Juliana's forehead and face every few minutes. My mother, generous as always, offers to pay for hotel rooms, but I make a couple of calls and learn that it would cost us five hundred dollars for a night's sleep. We decide, reluctantly, after some wavering, to make the long, dark, rainy drive back to Contigliano.

Angelo told us it wasn't difficult to get out of the city from here, and we think we might remember the way—across the bridge that leads out of Trastevere, across the river. So we climb back into the Kangoo, optimistically. And then . . . then we are lost in the heart of Rome on a wet Saturday night, with one sick child, one tired one, and three adults who've been pushed to the edge of their reserves of patience. We are not too proud to stop and ask directions. Following these directions with great care, we make a large rectangle around a stretch of the Tiber River, past the Vatican and back again. We stop and ask a second time and drive deeper into the heart of the city. Amanda points out familiar landmarks, optimistically. We have, well, we have a moment, Amanda and I. We pull up next to a *carabinieri* in traffic and he tells us to go left on the Lungotevere, when, as it will turn out ten minutes later, we should have gone right, and probably he knew that. I stop a fourth time, get out, run across another treacherous street hearing my mother say, "Be careful, Rol," as the car door closes. "Why?" I think. "Why bother?" Another gas station, a Bangladeshi attendant. "How do I get to the road for Rieti?" *La strada per Rieti,* it sounds so nice in Italian. He shrugs, points at his customers, a young couple filling up their car. I approach them, *La strada per Rieti?* The man defers to the woman. The woman starts to give directions, but the directions are complicated. The man corrects her. They have a little moment of their own; it is not a good night for loving couples in the Eternal City. After their exchange of words, the man says, "Just follow us." We follow them. Ten dark blocks later, they pull over, the young man gets out and explains that there is XX September Street, over there, right in front of us. It leads to the Salaria.

The Salaria leada to Rieti. Unfortunately, however, the roads here are all one-way, which is why his girlfriend was sending me halfway around the moon. He isn't sure exactly how to get onto XX September Street, heading north, but there it is, right over there, you can see it. I thank him and he and his girlfriend drive off.

We are, as the young man suspected, blocked from getting onto XX September Street by an interlocking web of one-way alleys that were comfortably wide enough for a couple of horses in the days when they were built, and then comfortably wide enough for one car before the human race discovered parking. We go toward XX September Street, tiredly, hopefully, and entangle ourselves deeper in the maze. Everyone is silent now, as if we are all infected, if not with the stomach flu, then at least with the part of Juliana's illness that has rendered her mute. We stop to ask a policeman—he is half-blocking the already half-blocked street, parked behind an unmarked Mercedes with a blue light on its roof. Some kind of raid has been going on; perhaps they are arresting the people who put up the one-way signs, or who designed this street, or who made access to XX September impossible. The raid must have been successful because the policeman is in a good mood. He smiles, looks at the faces in the Kangoo, tells us to take the next left, then the first left, then the next left after that. We do so and, in three more minutes, find ourselves right beside him again. He laughs. His colleague, one of two thick-forearmed detectives in the unmarked Mercedes says, "Follow me." And we do. We follow him for ten minutes. Left, right, left, left, left, left, right, right. He is speeding, going through lights as they turn red, changing lanes and making turns without signaling, having some fun, blowing off some steam after the stress of his drug raid. It is a kind of test: can the foreigner keep up with a true Italian man when it comes to breaking the laws of the road?

At last, test concluded, minimal passing grade given out, the detective comes to a screeching stop at a red light and waves us up beside him. His passenger is hanging one heavy arm out the window and grinning like a boy at a baseball game. He points to the entrance to the Salaria, just in front of us now, beyond the lights. "For Rieti," he says. "Just get on there, and—"

"*Sempre diritto,*" my mother says quietly in the back seat.

"*Sempre diritto*", the detective says happily. We thank him and start out on our wet, black, endless drive north. Everyone but my mother and me falls asleep. Juliana has not thrown up, on the one hand; on the other hand, she has not eaten. At last, finally, a vacation day in ruins behind us, we pull up the long narrow road past Agnese's place to our pretty house on the hill, and, as we are taking things out of the car, Amanda comes within a second, within an inch, of locking the keys in the house. It is a few degrees warmer inside than outside, that's all I'll say. Juliana throws up once more in the middle of the night. In my journal the next morning I make this entry: "We'll try to find a way to make the best of this."

11

The doctor at Bambin' Gesu had advised us that, if Juliana threw up once or twice more in the next day or so, not to worry, but that, if the vomiting showed no signs of abating, we should bring her back to the hospital and admit her. So Amanda and I and my mother and Alexandra are engaged in a vomit vigil, a regurgitation watch, observing our light-haired little gem, hoping she will begin to show the spark of humor and petulant independence she usually carries through this world.

The next day, Sunday morning, my mother and I drive down to the small stone church that stands by the side of the road a mile or so beyond Agnese's place. Because things are so unsettled at the cold house on the hill, we arrive twenty minutes late for Mass. The only seats open are near the front, so we tramp up the main aisle in the middle of the service and take our places, not very unobtrusively, I'm afraid, in the second row, left side.

The church is tiny, with newly stuccoed, whitewashed interior walls. There are flowers on the altar, and the priest is a stocky, likeable, sixty-year-old with a direct gaze and strong shoulders. The sermon is about marriage, that much I can understand. Something about patience and good will. Amanda and I have been married to each other almost half our lives. We have a good, peaceful marriage, but on occasion this peace is broken by the strains of our many travel adventures, by money worries, by our differing quirks and habits. We are not,

I suspect, alone in this. We always patch things up, and I'm sure that will happen again, here, once the stress of the situation lifts a bit. I lower my head and offer up a little petition for forgiveness. We give generously when the plate is passed; my mother goes up to communion. After the parting blessing— *Andate in pace*— everyone files out patiently into the rain, everyone except a woman in a full-length chinchilla coat. Having fulfilled her sacred obligation for the week, this woman pushes rudely past us and past some older folk, complaining loudly about the weather, as if it affects her and no one else, as if, for the rest of us, it is a sunny day, or the cold and drizzle don't matter, but for her, in her chinchilla and gold, it is an affront, a personal insult, an injustice to rival any of the great injustices of history.

As we are driving up the slick hill, we stop to say hello to Agnese, and Mimmo's wife Rita. They have gone to church, too, and are now on their way to the cemetery to visit the graves of relatives. There is only a little time before the cemetery closes, but they offer to come up and help us figure out why the washing machine isn't working (a real problem, with Juliana's soiled clothes). They tell us that there is, indeed, a terrible flu going around, and when we ask how long it lasts, they shake their heads, pucker their lips and speak words that cannot possibly be true: *"Sei, sette giorni."*

Six or seven days.

When they step into the house the first thing Rita says is, *"Mmm, fa caldo."* It's warm.

With the assistance of these nice women, we solve the puzzle of the incalcitrant *machina per la bucca*, and then, to celebrate that small victory, we decide to go down the hill and into Contigliano for lunch, and try out the other restaurant there, at the Hotel Vigne. There is no problem finding it, at least—a new white building with wooden window trim, set behind a

TAKING THE KIDS TO ITALY

large parking lot. But it seems to be closed. I step out of the
Kangoo and approach the entrance, and a man there tells me
brusquely that the restaurant is actually next door. We go next
door and step into an elegant looking place, all mirrors, wine
bottles, and thirty tables with salmon colored cloths and shining silver. We feed Juliana a sip of water and watch her closely.
She seems—please God—to be just a bit better. We ask the
waiter—a species of kind, enthusiastic, helpful young man that
populates the eateries of Italy like a legion of saints—if he can
make Juliana a plate of rice "without nothing." Not a problem.
The wine is very good. I feel like I am definitely coming down
with a cold, or the flu, and because of that, and because of the
way things have been going over the past couple of days, I immediately set about drinking too much of this particular vintage. Partly due to this indulgence, I allow the saintly waiter to
talk me into ordering an appetizer of pigskin and cannelloni
beans, though, as I do so, my mother and Amanda look at me
as if I have fallen completely over the edge of sanity.

In a few minutes our waiter proudly carries the dish out
from the kitchen. The beans are delicious, large and soft and
cooked in a thick sauce. I offer some all around; no takers. The
pigskin is tender and mucousy, thick inch-by-half-inch strips
that slide of their own power from the tip of the tongue down
the throat. No one else at the table appreciates the convenience
of this.

In the middle of this solitary preamble to our Sunday feast,
Juliana starts coughing in a familiar way. Amanda and I con-
verge on her from either side and hold napkins up to her
mouth just in time, and, after another cleaning job—bib,
sweater, pants, booster seat—I end up leaving most of the
mucousy pigskin in the bowl, hiding some of it under the last
of the beans so the waiter won't be offended.

From that point, through the remainder of the fair lunch at

Hotel Vigne, the remainder of that day, and all of that night, Amanda and I set our own small troubles aside; we are oppressed by worry for our daughter. We are caught in a kind of vice between the idea of making another four-hour round trip drive to Rome and waiting several hours in the emergency room of Bambin' Gesu, on the one hand, and the idea of not making that trip and running the risk of Juliana's illness turning worse, on the other. This kind of thing is one of the less talked about aspects of parenthood: the millions of decisions that must be made, and the weight and difficulty of those decisions. Let your child watch TV, or not let your child watch TV? And how often? And for how long? And which shows? Let your child eat sweets or not? Insist that she finish her broccoli, or not? Floss his teeth, or not? Brush after breakfast, or not? Wear a heavy coat or don't wear it? There is almost always an element of self-interest involved, something that is next to impossible to quash entirely: if she watches TV you will have peace in the house for an hour or so, you'll be able to get some work done, make a phone call to a friend, wash the dishes, cook supper, read a section of the paper. If he has chocolate, you won't have to listen to complaints and pleading; you will be admired and liked by one of the people who mean most to you in this world. If you decide to delay a second doctor's visit and just keep watching Juliana, you won't have to make the long trip to Rome again, won't have to sit behind the wheel for four hours, drive in Roman traffic, wait in the emergency room.

But then the shadow of guilt falls on you like a tree limb at a picnic. What if the long stretches in front of the TV harm her in some way? She'll be missing out on reading time. What if the chocolate gives her cavities? The pain for her and the expense for you. What if you don't go to Rome, and she gets really sick, and ends up in the hospital for a week, and catches some infection there, and you have to stay nearby at one of the 250-Euro a night hotels? What if something worse than that happens, something inconceivable, beyond terrible, and what if it is your fault?

Amanda and I are usually pretty good about these things. We have similar ideas about the philosophy of raising children, and this makes for a general harmony at home. We walk a happy line between the most authoritarian parents, who solve various domestic dilemmas by instilling fear in their kids and turning them into army privates who must salute before sitting down, straight-backed, to their gruel and stale bread; and the most lenient, whose kids can spit on the floor and curse the neighbors and play their music so loud the walls shake . . . and hear only the mildest, most polite requests for obedience. ("Olivia, sweetheart, Mom and Dad want to share with you that it doesn't actually feel good for us when you drive the car into the side of the house.")

We're usually a good team, but on this afternoon, one member of the team takes a short recess. Like most all fathers and mothers, I simply can't bear to see my children suffer. And my response to this parental dilemma, to this particular stretch of suffering, is to have so much of the wine at the Hotel Vigne that, when lunch is finished and we are heading out, Amanda has to get behind the wheel. I am not drunk, not at all. I am not the kind of man who gets drunk on four or five glasses of wine. I am just . . . temporarily insulated from the realities of the day.

Amanda drives us up to the old part of the city, a knot of gray stone buildings that leans over the rest of Contigliano as if it might topple down onto the Food Co-op at the first shake of the country's famously capricious tectonic plates. The ancient streets, cobbled with fist-sized stones, were made for burros, not autos (not even Kangoos), and are so slick from the cold morning rain that the car skids and backslides and she barely makes it up the spiraling road into a hundred-foot-square parking area in front of Saint Cecelia's church. We would like to visit the church, but its front doors are locked. A light cold rain is still falling. Perfect walking-around weather with sick kids. But we have few other good options. Juliana sits sleepily in the stroller, draped in blankets, and we walk along Contigliano's stone paths, with the stone houses seeming to strain in toward each other above our heads like yearning lovers, and the doors and windows silent and wet. It is as if we have stepped through a magical portal and deep into the dreary past.

We come upon the remains of a church, roofless now, built, according to a plaque attached to one stone wall, in 1428. Even in my semi-depressed, partly-inebriated state, this number makes an impression. 1428. Five hundred and seventy-five years ago. A lifetime before Columbus. There is no ceiling left, not even any wooden beams, only a stone floor and two and a half sides, the semi-enclosed interior offering a view down over the misty, pretty valley. There is a primitive, almost pagan feel to this space: you know people prayed here, but there are no candles, sacred texts, or stained glass saints to link you to them, only the harsh, wet, sloping walls built by hand a half millennium ago. There is no softness to God here, at this moment, no ease, no comfort, no slack to be cut.

On the way back to the car we pass two stooped older women, dressed in black, paying a Sunday visit to a friend. I practice my Italian on them. "Is the weather always this bad here?" I say, and the more gregarious of the women answers: "God forbid!" She tells us that this part of the city was built in the thirteenth century, and the other part in the sixteenth, and I want to pass the marvel of that on to our kids. But they embody the passage of time, the string of humanity leading back and back and forward and forward; no sense in talking to them about it. These elderly women know that they were just like

88

our girls seventy years ago, that the girls will probably be similar to them seventy years hence, but who can say it? To the younger part of that balanced equation especially, who can say what has to be said about the rough, exhilarating passage that is a human life?

We bid the women good-day and walk back toward the car. As we are making our second pass by the church we come up-on a man sweeping grains of rice away from the front door—we remember seeing a wedding procession coming down out of the old part of the city as we were driving to the Hotel Vigne. This man looks up from his work and, without any prompting from us, invites us in.

The interior of St. Cecelia's is dim and cool. As our eyes adjust we see that there are three gilded altars, one in front and one on each side, and the shadows and high, vaulted ceiling give the interior a different kind of sacred feel, as if a warmer God has been captured here in the sweet, smoky air. The wedding, the sermon about marriage, the way Amanda and I tussle and reconcile when we travel—that subject seems to be surrounding us these days, and I always think about such things in churches, anyway: if religion isn't at least partly about learning to live with people, how can it matter?

There is an old organ perched above a small choir loft on the rear wall, made of carved chestnut, is my guess. Still just a bit voluble from the wine, I tell the caretaker how marvelous I think it is, and he says: "Do you play? I'll turn it on for you."

Where else does this happen? Does it happen in Massachusetts, in Chicago, in L.A? At home, ever, on your best day, do you walk into a church and see a three-hundred-year-old organ and have someone offer to let you touch it, let alone play it?

I don't play, can't—two years of piano lessons in my teens don't qualify me to lay a finger on this musical treasure—but we want to get a close-up view of the organ anyway so our new friend opens a tiny door and Amanda, Alexandra, and I climb up a two-foot-wide, winding, creaking stairway to the choir loft while my mother pushes Juliana back and forth down below. From our precarious perch there, it seems to me, as it sometimes does in old churches, that I can feel the woodworkers, plasterers, masons and sculptors at work, feel the millions of prayers that have been offered up from this building—during weddings and wars, famines and funerals and festivals. We examine the organ in a kind of awe, and then stand for a while in the loft, letting our eyes run over the shadowy pews below.

Downstairs again, we are offered a guided tour. St. Cecelia's is a modest establishment, by Italian standards: it took only sixty years to build. The caretaker tells us it suffered some damage in the earthquake of 1998, and that the government is now paying for it to be restored. "You were in that earthquake," I say to Alexandra, after the caretaker has led us back down the creaking steps and given us a tour of the basement catacombs. "Mommy and you and I were in Orvieto. Mom was out taking photographs and I was in the hotel room with you on the second floor, and you were asleep on the bed when the whole building started to shake."

I had never been in an earthquake, but I somehow sensed that it wasn't normal, even in Orvieto, for buildings to tremble. So I picked Alexandra up and stood in the doorway because it seemed to me I remembered reading something about that being the safest place. The quake passed, nothing but a mild tremor in those parts. In Assisi, fifty miles away, a church roof collapsed and four worshippers died.

Because the only other option is to return to the cool house, we decide, once our tour of St. Cecelia's is finished and we've expressed our gratitude to the kindly caretaker, to drive over to Rieti for dessert. The rain has stopped but the air stays damp and full of chill. I have a bad cold, that's obvious now, maybe even some kind of flu. It occurs to me that, sitting for all those hours in Bambin' Gesu, I might have caught whatever it is that has been tormenting Juliana and half the children in Rome. But that would be too much bad luck for one week. Italy would never do that to me. God would never do it. I shake the foolish thought away.

We make the twenty-minute drive and have a short, cold walking tour of Rieti. It's a hilly, stony place with some character—dark facades and cobbled streets. The light from gleaming bookshops and stores selling scarves and purses pours out onto the sidewalks, casting a little brightness into a gloomy day. At one point we stumble upon a weird, imitation-American festival where men and women dressed as cowboys are doing something that vaguely resembles a square dance in front of an outdoor stage. I think: These are the lengths people will go to for entertainment on cold days in this part of the country. But I don't say it.

We end up taking refuge in a *pasticceria* where a soccer game is blasting on the TV, a few people are wandering around licking ice cream cones, and the headlines on a stack of newspapers read: "Two Setbacks for U.S. in War Preparations." As I am holding Juliana in my arms near the counter where the brioches and cookies are sold, she starts to cough. I take her outside, where she throws up again. I clean her, while the others enjoy their ice cream in peace, and soon we leave Rieti to make the short drive back across the plain, talking about going to Rome the next morning, full of dread, wondering if it is safe even to wait that long.

But the next morning we wake up to the sound of happy young voices—two of them—knocking against the tile floors. It is not sunny outside the windows, but the house is a bit warmer than it has been. Maybe the worst of our bad luck has past. Surely it has.

91

12

Another wonderful Italian spring day: 45 degrees and damp, with fog lying across our valley like the smoke from burning dreams. Our options are: sit in the cool house and read and watch TV while the kids grow increasingly restless. Or drive to Spoleto, which one of our guide books calls "Perhaps the most beautiful of the Italian hill towns."

So we drive to Spoleto. By some miracle, some intercession of the spirits of the Umbrian hills, this ninety-minute trip is without incident. No one throws up. We don't get lost—even winding through the factory district of Terni, following signs. Though there are traces of snow on the higher hills we have to cross, the roads are not slick, the blue arrow signs that read SPOLETO are easy to follow. Shortly before noon we see the Ponte del Torre, Spoleto's famous concrete bridge, built in the 14th century on top of Roman aqueducts. Its enormous looping arches are the signature of the city, and we pull off the highway there and try to find the center of town.

Strangely enough, Spoleto seems to have no center. Its main road curves and climbs, up and up, passing through short commercial strips of three or four stores and bars in front of which we almost park, then decide not to. Eventually we follow signs to the Duomo—Spoleto's Romanesque cathedral—park on a steep street in front of it (Good sign: the clutch of the Kangoo no longer smells when I go backwards up a hill.)

and ask someone where we might find a restaurant. Good sign number two: Juliana is singing, "Bah Bah Black Sheep".

The first restaurant we come across has no high chair and a limited menu, so we end up in a place presided over by a raven-haired hostess with film-star looks. There is one other customer—a grumpy, suit-wearing, septuagenarian spooning soup carefully into his mouth at a nearby table. At least he's not smoking. Whatever the trials of marriage and fatherhood might be on any given day, they pale in comparison to the picture of this man's lonely life—his perfect posture and well-tailored clothes, the obvious sorrow with which he brings spoon to mouth. Even the exceptionally friendly waitress, carrying over his main course, seems to keep a small distance, as if the man has a kind of loneliness flu that one might catch.

Both Alexandra and Juliana love to see food being prepared, so I lead them to the edge of a sparkling, modern kitchen where the chef looks up from his work and smiles at the girls with pasta dough draped over both hands. I wonder if something of that smile can be passed on, via the semolina, to the soup-eating man, and I offer up a small prayer of thanks— because Juliana seems to have recovered, because we all seem to have recovered, because we are able to travel, because we have people we can share a meal with on a cool spring day.

My mother orders a bowl of vegetable soup, which proves to be quite delicious. Amanda goes with the mixed grill. Pasta for Alexandra, rice for Ju Ju Be. *Pappardelle al cinghale* for the adventurous, slightly woozy now, member of the group. This seems to be the week of the pig because *cinghale* is the word for wild boar. The *pappardelle*, wide ribbons of pasta, are a foot long, and the sauce has small chips of black olives in it, and a pleasant wild-tasting spice, and the wine is passable, drinkable. I should probably note here, with all this talk of wine, that I barely know a cabernet from a merlot. At home, I buy a bottle of white and a bottle of red every week and limit myself to one glass at dinner, telling myself it's good for the arteries. When friends visit, Amanda has a glass, and I have two. The bottles rarely cost more than fifteen dollars; we sit around joking about the vocabulary of wine connoisseurs. But I enjoy the taste of it, and enjoy the sense-connection to my childhood, when my father's parents started us off at a young age with strong red wine mixed with a little orange soda, then gradually increased the wine and decreased the soda until, by the time we were in high school, our glasses were all a deep crimson. My grandfather made his own wine, in fact, and one of the strongest sense-memories of my childhood is walking into what he called his "wine-cellar" a tiny room in the back of the basement where he kept two wooden kegs that were twice the size of the younger grandchildren. The cobwebs, the dust and spiders, the musty, vinegary smell, the sight of the old oak barrels with their rusted metal belts and vaguely illicit aura—my fascination with wine began there, and I am content now simply to enjoy it, to know the decent from the indecent vintage, and to leave it at that.

We have some *brocoletta*, too, pleasingly bitter, then add more numbers to the credit card balance, bid the hostess and cook good-bye, nod to the sad solitary man, and wander down into another pocket of shops for coffee and dessert, served to us in a narrow bar by a six-foot-tall woman with an attitude.

Afterwards, inside the cathedral, which was consecrated in 1198, we find a gaggle of Belgian school kids who speak English better than I do, and an absolutely fantastic fresco above the altar, painted by Fra Lippo Lippi (who died in this building, at work on another masterpiece, and is buried here). In the elaborate scene, Mary is being chosen to be the mother of Jesus, and she is kneeling beside a stern king. Angels bear witness from either side. Above them Lippo Lippi has set a rainbow-covered sky, bands of color running through it in arcs, impossibly beautiful blues and greens, a vision of heaven. We stand for a long time and look at it, with Juliana's happy voice banging against the walls, and the schoolgirls getting an art history lecture from their teacher—the boys getting a biology lesson from studying the schoolgirls—and Alexandra and my mother playing some kind of discreet hide and seek near the confessionals.

Late in the afternoon, all our appetites—food, art, spiritual nourishment, hide-and-seek—having been calmed, we leave Spoleto and make the simple, straightforward drive back to Contigliano. It has been a good day, at least in relation to the days that preceded it.

But then, on the simple and straightforward drive back to Contigliano, we become tremendously lost.

It is difficult to explain how this happens. I am driving, Amanda is navigating—the usual arrangement. We follow the same road we took that morning, make it safely through Terni for the second time. South of Terni, there is a road to the right marked "Contigliano", but we know enough by now not to take that road, because there is a quicker way just ahead.

Everything would be fine, except that somehow, by some evil magic, the second turnoff to Contigliano never makes itself visible to us. I know that the shorter road must be there because we took it on the way north. But on the way south it is not there, simply not there. We end up taking the *third* Contigliano exit—tired now, all of us. We've spent three hours in the car again today, I'm sick, Juliana might be recovering, the weather has turned overcast, cold, and depressing—and the third road brings us, somehow, not to Contigliano but to the other side, the eastern side, of the vast plain. Somehow there are all these hills beyond the plain, hills with switchback curves. Just the thing for a driver coming down with the stomach flu, and his oldest daughter who gets motion sickness on a curving driveway. "I'm not feeling good," Alexandra says from the back seat. My mother is silent. Juliana has begun to cry and say, "Out! OUT!" every ten seconds. Perhaps we should take that as a good sign—Ju Ju Be back to her old feisty self—but we don't. Amanda is studying the map. "I see where we are," she says. I do, too, because, in the far western distance, miles and miles away, the town of Contigliano shines in an errant ray of sunlight.

This is beautiful landscape: interwoven hills and cultivated fields with small stone houses here and there. Too bad I'm not in a mood to appreciate it. Amanda wants to stop and photograph. I pull over onto the edge of a farmer's field, and we wait there while she has a few minutes to herself with a camera. Anxious though I am to get home, it does feel good not to be moving, and to give my hardworking wife a moment of peace in which she can indulge her art.

We are at the end of the afternoon. From time to time the sun peeks out from beneath thick rain clouds, and, as we start moving again and close in on the edges of Rieti, it throws a rainbow up in front of us, as if in echo of the fresco in Spoleto. Maybe Fra Lippo Lippi got lost near here one morning on the way to the *duomo*, and his wife wanted to step out of the horse-drawn cart and admire the scenery, and he felt like throwing up, with his kids in back complaining . . . and it inspired him to make his masterpiece.

But, sitting behind the wheel, wanting only to be in bed, I am visited by a different sort of inspiration. Ill and road-weary, I understand now, too late, what I should have realized at home: our vacation is going to consist of three and four-hour trips to interesting (to the adults) hill cities in the cold center of Italy. The girls will quickly tire of it. The adults will end up exhausted, not refreshed, at the end of a month of this. In these high hills, it only makes sense that spring is going to arrive later than it will in other parts of Italy, and spring is what we came for. It only makes sense that the most beautiful hill towns in Italy aren't exactly a kid's idea of paradise. I see my mistake now, see it as clearly as I see the old part of Contigliano off there in the distance, beyond the rainbow. The problem isn't our decision to come to Italy in February and March. The problem is that we came to the *wrong part* of Italy in February and March. At one point we'd been considering a trip to Lecce, (pronounced "lech" as in "lecher" and "chay" as in "chamber") in the heel of the boot, way down south. We'd read about it, talked to some friends who'd been there. Into the tired mind of a man who wants only peace and comfort for himself and his family slips another brilliant inspiration: Lecce, of course; that's where we should have gone. I decide to discuss Lecce with Amanda, that same night, once the girls are in bed and this sour feeling in my head has passed.

When we finally make it back to Contigliano, we stop in at the town's modest library to read our emails on their only computer. There we talk to the young librarian and mention Juliana's illness. "Oh yes," she says. "My son had it for three or four days. And I had it too."

"Adults can get this?"

"Oh, yes," she says. "Some adults can. It can go on quite a long time."

My stomach suddenly doesn't feel right. Alexandra and Juliana are restless, so, as Amanda answers a friend's message, and my mother browses the magazines, I take the girls out for a stroll in the cold night. Juliana is badly in need of a diaper change, so I accomplish it there, on the hood of the Kangoo, masterfully, with Alexandra holding a blanket around her younger sister to keep the cold wind away. Quick as a pit crew changing tires, barely a cry from our recovering child. I take the rolled-up diaper and deposit it in a barrel and along with it, somehow, that fast, go my hopes for our Contigliano dream.

On the way up the dark winding road to the house, we startle a family of porcupines and they turn and fluff out their quills at us, strange sight in the headlights, perhaps some kind of omen.

That night, before dinner, Alexandra watches the *Sound of Music* and Juliana wanders around handing out potato chips, like her old self. But when they and my mother are in bed, Amanda and I have a little talk. We are not the kind of people who can't admit to having made a mistake. Both of us had been equally enthusiastic about Contigliano—though my enthusiasm was the driving force for getting us here. But now, after this first week, both of us see very clearly that what seemed to us, in America, like an intriguing and restful vacation in the Italian heartland, seemed that way because we were using our pre-parent minds. We were thinking about the trip the way we thought about trips before Alexandra and Juliana were born, or when they were so small and portable that it really didn't make any difference to them where we went. We were remembering good meals and fine museums, drives through countryside we'd never seen, visits to ancient villages with ancient churches in them, discussions with interesting and warmhearted Italians. But the factor we had left out of our calculations was this: none of that means anything to a child. We see that now, with a painful clarity. The question is: what to do about it? When we've talked for a while, put our resourceful, adventurous, travel-loving minds together, we get out the map, spread it across the dinner table, and calculate the distance to Lecce: 389.3 miles.

<u>13</u>

The next day, of course, because we've taken the outrageous step of deciding to abandon the cold Contigliano house without having stayed there even a week, the sun shines brilliantly into the large room. The temperature spikes to fifty-five degrees. Too late, I've already called Lecce and talked to a contact at the university there; we've already asked her to find us an apartment for a week, with the option of staying another week if we like the city. My cold, flu, or whatever it is, has grown worse.

Mimmo appears in his three-wheeled jalopy, and begins making a cover for the stone fireplace in the center of the house, "so all the heat doesn't escape", he says. I like him better now. It's not so much that he is grumpy as somber, without a lot of affect, but he is a decent man, a twinkle of wry humor behind his words. When I tell him what a beautiful country Italy is, he says, *"Si, ma tutti i ladri."* Yes, but full of thieves. When I tell him we will be going to Lecce the next day, and probably won't be coming back, he recites this classic and memorable line: *"A Lecce fa piu freddo."* In Lecce, it's even colder.

But I don't believe him. Lecce, "the Florence of the South" according to our guide book, is four hundred miles closer to the equator than where we now stand. I can't think of a country in either hemisphere where you can drive four hundred miles closer to the equator, to a city at sea level, and find colder weather.

After breakfast we all go out into the sunshine and let it fall on the bare skin of our arms and faces. "This is the best day of vacation!" Alexandra sings down into the valley. My mother and I hit golf balls off the lawn into a rocky field, aiming for the light post there as if it is a flagstick on a green.

Everything seems fine and wonderful again, except that Amanda takes Juliana for a ride to Greccio so she will fall asleep, shoots a few photos there, and when they return, Juliana is dull-eyed and listless all over again, as she was on the first day of her illness. She eats two bites of hot dog and has a terrible attack of diarrhea. We go back to the library to send some emails and the diarrhea problems continue. I won't go into detail. We make another pit-stop diaper-change. I walk over to the *farmacia* and explain the situation. "There is a medicine that works well for children with diarrhea," the attendant there tells me. "But we can't give it to you without a prescription."

"Is there a doctor's office nearby?"

"Yes," she says, "but the doctor isn't in today. There's another doctor in town, I don't know about that one. His office is near the Co-Op."

We walk up the hill, past the Co-op and into the edges of the old section, find the second doctor's office, knock, ring the bell. No answer. Not today. Lecce, I am thinking. There would be doctors at home today if we were in Lecce. There would be something interesting for the kids to do, a first-class golf course, a warm house.

All of us are unnerved by our bad luck so far, but a bit surprised at ourselves that we've decided on such a radical evacuation. Alexandra is particularly upset. She is a person who forms attachments to places and things, doesn't like to throw away clothes that no longer fit her, or dolls she no longer touches, doesn't want friends to move, ever, has made me promise, on a number of occasions, that we will never move from our home in Massachusetts. Or that, if we do, we will never actually sell the house.

"Stinky old Italy," she says, as we're loading ourselves back into the Kangoo.

"Stinky old Italy? I thought you liked it here. I thought this was the best day of our vacation."

"Well," she says, "Not so bad stinky old Italy."

On the way back up the road we cross paths with Mimmo, coming downhill in his little truck. We shake hands and say good-bye, and I feel like I've had a fifteen-minute blind date with his sister and decided not to call again. This is his place, his territory, and we've barely given it a chance. On the one hand, I suppose it makes us the spoiled Americans, forever embracing and discarding new dreams in the hopes of soothing ourselves with some impossible perfection. But hurting Mimmo's feelings—if, in fact, we have done that—or offending Agnese, Molly, or the owner of the house, isn't half as important to me as seeing a certain kind of traveling happiness on the face of my children, wife, and mother. We've come a long way to see that shine, spent a lot of money we probably shouldn't have spent. It's been clear from the first cold night that coming to Contigliano in late winter, with two young children, was a foolish mistake. We could stay and try to make the best of that, or we could listen to the seductive whisper of the road again, put our chips on a risky bet, and hope for better luck.

In my journal that night, as we're packing up and preparing to go, I write, "My tendency to glamorize Italy may have been permanently damaged." But of course that isn't so.

14

The next morning, Juliana is listless again at breakfast.
Usually she has the appetite of an infantryman in basic training—three bowls of cereal, a whole apple, toast, crackers—but
today she takes only a couple of mouthfuls of cereal and says,
"Down, down."

My mother keeps the girls occupied while Amanda and I
spend two hours packing up, cleaning up, washing the bedclothes and turning all gauges, levers, knobs, and dials back to
what we remember as their original positions. As I'm gathering
our things I pick up one of Alexandra's dolls, a miniature Dor-
othy from *The Wizard of Oz*. I accidentally squeeze her belly
and—this is absolutely true—she squeaks out the only sen-
tence she knows: "There's no place like home. There's no place
like home."

For some reason—maybe they sense our impending departure—Agnese's aggressively friendly mongrels have come up
the hill again to pay us a visit, en masse, and it's all we can do
to keep them out of the house whenever we open the door to
carry out another suitcase. I look at Lecce on the map and
think: it looks warm there; it looks interesting; we'll be able to
walk out our door and be in a city rather than having to drive
everyplace. The ocean is nearby; the guidebook says there is a
good eighteen-hole golf course a short distance away. The cities we want to visit will be only half an hour away, not two

hours, not three. I am doing what I always do when I look at maps: imagining paradise.

Shortly after ten o'clock we finish packing the Kangoo and start off down the bumpy road. At Agnese's I get out to hand over the keys. She seems unsurprised. *"La casa e' molto isolata,"* she says kindly, and I say it's a beautiful house, but yes, isolated, and the girls haven't been feeling well. She is sorry to hear that, tells me about her own daughter—who died after a motorcycle crash, age 16—and her husband, who died from cancer a few years back. She says there is no feeling on earth worse than the feeling of worrying about your children's health. "But I have serenity," she says. And it seems to me that she does.

We head south. One last drive through Contigliano, one last trip across the pretty plain and through the outskirts of Rieti. This time, as if the curse has been lifted, we find the road we're looking for—toward a place called Avezzano—without any trouble, and begin the scenic drive down Italy's spine, with the snowy four, five, and seven-thousand-foot mountains for company. Somewhere in the first part of that drive I say to Amanda, "I'm feeling a little flu-ish."

"Me, too," she says. "My stomach isn't right. Maybe it was the eggs Agnese gave us."

"Maybe."

As far as Avezzano on State Highway 578 we encounter no problems, though I'm feeling worse by the mile and stop twice, the first time for a breath of fresh air, and the second for a dose of ibuprofen. In the back seat, my mother is teaching Alexandra a card game called "Snap!" I do not know how this game is played, I know only that when someone puts down a certain card she has to yell out SNAP! At top volume and slap the back of her grandmother's hand. I had three hours of sleep last night. With each beautiful, mountainous mile it's becoming clearer that what I'm feeling has nothing to do with Agnese's fresh eggs—which Amanda scrambled for breakfast. No, the bitter truth is that I'm sinking into the influenzal muck Juliana is just climbing out of. I remember that I had a bad visit to the bathroom that morning as we were packing up. I remember that, on our first evening in the house we mistakenly took our drinking water right from the faucet and only later found out it wasn't potable. SNAP! The road winds. SNAP! Juliana stirs, coughs in a way I don't like. Amanda takes off her seatbelt and turns around to look at her, but she goes back to sleep.

We find Avezzano with no trouble, and then, somehow, despite the fact that Mimmo—who drove a truck on these roads for thirty years—advised us that the best route to Lecce was the Autostrada from Avezzano to the Adriatic coast, Amanda and I decide on a different, more inland road that continues down through the mountains. I have no explanation for this, no defense. Between the two of us, we have a tremendous amount of travel experience, we've read a lot of maps, we are not stupid or especially proud people. According to our map it just looks like the better way to go, that's all I can say. We head off toward Benevento, planning to spend the night there at an excellent *agriturismo* that exists in my imagination.

But south of Avezzano, on glorious Highway 17, things go very bad very quickly. I have promised the passengers that we will stop in the first good-sized town we see, and have lunch there. But there is no good-sized town after Avezzano, unless you count Sulmona, which, for reasons lost to me now, we don't like. I'm feeling worse and worse, some kind of pres-sure in the head, an awful buzzing sourness in my belly. Juliana is awake and crying. Alexandra yells, "SNAP!" We wind through the old gray mountains of the province of Abruzzo and, at last, come upon a good-sized town that meets our aesthetic stand-ards. Testa del Abruzzo.

"Lunch, coming up!" I say, through the miserable fog of

my illness. The cheerful dad. Lunch, coming up.

"Yay! Lunch!"

Testa del Abruzzo is a moderately attractive town, set tight on a hillside with forested mountain slopes in all directions. The streets are straight for only a few meters at a stretch, the stone houses stand in orderly curving rows, and it is clearly the type of place that draws a lot of tourists and abounds in good *trattorie*. Just after we come into town, the main road snakes around a corner, between houses so close on either side that we feel we can reach right in through someone's window and steal a loaf of bread. Beyond the first corner the narrow road winds a bit more, and then suddenly leads out into the mountain wilderness again.

"There has to be a restaurant in that town," I say. "We must have missed it. People there have to eat."

I let the *carabinieri* behind us go past, then, once the police car is out of sight, make a U-turn on the tight road. We glide back down the hill into Testa del Abruzzo. A man is working in his garage there, cutting wood, door open. I stop and ask about restaurants *qui vicino*, half expecting him to look at the children, at my mother, ask us where we're from and invite us upstairs for home-cooked pasta. But that's a scene from another dream. "There's a restaurant just around this next corner," he says, unsmiling, all business, focused on the boards at hand. "But no place to leave your car."

"Can we leave it here?" I ask him.

He pauses half a beat and says, "No."

So we go around the hairpin corner again, and see, just where the amicable wood-cutter said they would be, signs for a *trattoria*. And, just as he said, there is no place to park anywhere in the vicinity. We drive slowly on. Half a mile further down the road is a bar with a three-car parking area in front and some disaffected youth hanging out there on the steps of a stone church. "Why are they smoking, Dad?" Alexandra wants to know.

I think: Because there is no hope of eating.

The bar itself is presided over by a kind, plump woman who leans down, smiles at the girls, and happily points the way to the bathrooms. We ask if it would be possible to get a dish of pasta here, but she says no, *sfortunatamente*, only drinks, brioches, candy bars. I want something more substantial for my girls and for Beetlebah. But it seems that I am in one of those streaks where every decision is the wrong one. This happens to me sometimes, even at home. I'll cruise along beautifully for days, writing the sentences I want to write, putting the kids to bed with just the right words, having one fruitful conversation after the next with my agent, my editor, picking the four-iron instead of the five-iron out of the bag to stroke my Titleist up onto the green. And then it will all go sour, all of it, all at once, in a cascade of failed judgment and foolishness and pure rotten luck. For me, because of some misalignment of the stars or some odd past-life karma, the good and the bad come bunched together in long stretches: on the day my first novel was accepted, after twelve years of writing, I came home to a letter from the Massachusetts State Lottery commission telling me I'd won $400 on my season ticket. On the day my father died, unexpectedly, I was immersed in a house painting project so poorly estimated that I was halfway through six weeks of working for nothing.

The bad stretches are as unnerving as the good ones are exhilarating; for the past few days now I've been thinking about this, a bruised, scratched-up man standing waist-deep in heavy surf watching the next enormous wave roll in. I ask the woman behind the little bar in Testa del Abruzzo what the other options for lunch might be, and she tells us about a restaurant, half a mile back, at the corner.

"But no place to park," I say.

"Right."

"Could we leave our car out front, here, and walk?"

"The police will come by," she says. "Give you a ticket."

"How much would the ticket be?"

"Sixty Euros," she says, and it is testimony to the state of my health—mental and physical—that I stand there for a few seconds wondering whether or not it's worth it. Sixty Euros, seventy bucks, let's see . . .

Outside, the disaffected youth are focusing all their wandering attention upon us, this naive-looking family of five with a fully-packed car. My laptop rests conspicuously in the back window of the Kangoo. Golf clubs beside it. Altogether it is a few thousand dollars' worth of merchandise, enough to keep them in cigarettes and nose rings for years.

"Let's drive on," I say. "There's bound to be a restaurant along the highway."

No one objects, so we load ourselves back into the car—Ma in the middle, the girls to either side, well strapped in, Amanda in the passenger seat, beneath a pile of maps, crackers, sippy-cups, notepads, plastic earrings, crayons and tissues. Yours truly behind the wheel. We wind away through the Abruzzan hills, this cold, rugged terrain to which so many Italian American families can trace their roots. A hundred years ago, before the wars, before Mussolini, before a complicated amalgam of foreign aid and social, political, and economic changes brought southern Italy into the modern world, the mountain towns of Abruzzo offered little or nothing in the way of upward mobility. Poor, bleak, disease-ridden, presided over by corrupt officials and choked by a rigid caste system, this land was the perfect breeding ground for a dream pronounced "America." What strong, smart, ambitious young man or woman, hearing the claims of gold and milk and honey, dreaming dreams of freedom and equality, would *not* have been tempted to pack up a few belongings, ride a horse-drawn cart to Naples, and book passage for the land of opportunity? It occurs to me that I am the inheritor of those kinds of inflated dreams, only in reverse. It's not gold I think about when I think about this land across the ocean, but warmth, unadulterated food, beautiful churches and sublime works of art, a slow-paced, family-oriented way of living. It's not property and kin I've abandoned in search of those dreams, only a cold house and a stack of bills, but there is a link, I can feel it. Some kind of genetic predisposition to the pursuit of a better life.

Not far outside Testa del Abruzzo we see a sign for a restaurant, the familiar crossed knife and fork, and the word *RISTORANTE*, unmistakable, beneath it. The sign instructs us to take the next right turn. We do that, and find ourselves with the highway at our back and a DO NOT ENTER sign in front of us. There are no other roads. The options are either to back up into the right-hand lane of the highway, or go forward against the flow of traffic. We back up onto the highway, retrace our route, take the right again, thinking we must have missed something. And there, in front of us, clear as day, is: DO NOT ENTER.

We drive on.

By this point it would be difficult to exaggerate how bad I'm feeling. Ugly little chills run up and down the skin of my arms and back like writhing snakes. Quick fevers come and go. And an awful, a sickening, a terrible sourness thrums in my belly and throat. "You feeling bad?" I say to Amanda.

"I was. It passed."

"Feeling okay, Mum?" I ask over my shoulder.

"My stomach was a little upset but it's better."

"You guys hungry back there?"

"Yeah, yeah."

Another two miles down the highway and we see a second RISTORANTE sign. This one points us left, and, full of hope, we climb a short steep driveway toward what appears to be a small hotel. It is one-thirty, exactly the middle of the Italian lunch hour, perfect timing. But when we crest the hill at the top of the drive we see that the windows of the hotel are boarded up, the small parking lot strewn with glass and litter. "Maybe drive around back," says my wonderful wife, Queen of Optimism.

To please her, I drive around behind the obviously abandoned place, then make a U-turn, muttering, sinking, and head back down.

"I'm real, real hungry, Dad," Alexandra says from the back seat.

On the highway again we see graffiti spray-painted on the abutment of an overpass: "GOD IS".

Another ten miles. Another small town. We take the exit and climb. I suppose that, in better moments, this would be a pretty place, an old fortified medieval town high above a tributary of the Sangro river with the mountains close in on all sides. But I am truly sick now and in the foulest of moods. Amanda directs me up a steep, impossibly narrow alleyway as if squeezing the Kangoo between those stone facades is the simplest thing in the world, and I SNAP! At her. There are a couple of inches clearance beyond the right and left mirrors. The alley makes a sharp left. I have to go back and forth several times to negotiate the corner. Juliana is screaming "UP! UP! UP ON MOMMY!" I feel very much like vomiting.

We crest the hill and the road opens into a small town square with an old church above us and a view of the river a few hundred feet below. Not a restaurant to be seen. Needing a moment by myself and a breath or two of air, I get out, walk over to the railing and wonder which would be the better plan:

to throw myself off now; or to wait, find a place for lunch, have one last good meal, and then throw myself off. I see a man, a very tiny man, walking past, and ask him about the chances of finding a place to eat in this town. He is most helpful. He leans his small body in toward me, looks at me out of the tops of his eyes, and his face is shining with good will. He talks very slowly and deliberately, wanting to get it right, and I have a sinful urge to lift him off his feet and fling him over the railing, down three hundred feet into the tributary of the River of Blood. I am not a violent man, but I have a terrible vision of myself picking him up and throwing him.

"There is a restaurant close by." He gestures, for some reason, at the church. "But it's closed. There's another one," he gestures off in the other direction, down the hill, "but I think they only serve dinner. You might try it." A friend of his is walking by. I am staring down toward the river in a hypnosis of malaise. I spit. The small man stays close to me, asks his friend about a third restaurant, and this man, too, comes up helpfully, looks at me and says, happily, *"Chiuso."* Closed. I turn and stare at the faces of the people I love, pressed against the glass of the Kangoo, keeping me on this earth, keeping me out of an Italian prison. At this point a third man walks up, my size, a bit larger, leans in close, and says, "Are you from France?"

I want to throw them all over, every one of them, large and small, then jump over after them.

A fourth man walks past. My little pal calls out to him about helping this hungry family from America find some lunch. Feeding the Merullos has become a community project. "Try the *Locanda*," he calls back.

"No, no, the *Locanda* isn't open, fool."

"Sure it is. I just walked by there."

"Try the *Locanda* then," the small man says, turning his face up to me again, helpfully, eagerly, kindly. And he gives me

110

complicated directions I half listen to.

On the way to the *Locanda*, we get lost, of course, but not very lost. Dogs greet us outside, possibly the same dogs we made friends with at the house in Contigliano. They have followed us down Highway 17, wanting another shot at the tires of the stalled Kangoo. Inside the *Locanda*, it is very cold, and the owner isn't particularly friendly, his food not particularly good. It's not a surprise to me that we are the only customers. Juliana eats nothing. My mother wraps herself in her coat and eventually sits on the upright radiator until the man rudely tells her not to, she might break it. It's only made of steel, after all; and she's what, all of a hundred and ten pounds? I cannot report what Amanda does because, by this point, we are not really making eye contact. It is my fault, all my fault, completely my fault . . . and I am certainly doing penance. I have a few bites of gnocchi with some *brocoletta* mixed in, and immediately feel I'm going to throw it up all over the *Locanda's* cold tile floor and fragile radiators. I summon all my willpower. Must go on. We pay. In our never ending attempt to improve our language skills, we ask the owner what "*locanda*" means. Money in his hand, he is slightly less unfriendly and, after struggling a bit, helps us to understand that the word means something like "inn."

We leave the inn. We must go on. Outside, the pack of mongrels pests, circles, jumps up on the girls, yaps and yips. Alexandra shrieks, I shoo them off. They are dealing with the wrong man, at the wrong time. One scratch, one bit of broken skin on either one of my girls and I will slaughter the pesky canines there in the town square, slaughter them, skewer them, cook them well done and bring them over to the *Locanda* to be served as the evening special.

Foul, foul, foul mood.

Juliana has had another terrible diarrhea, so Amanda and I

111

change her in the cold wind, on a park bench, with the dogs, unflappable, unafraid, unaware that they're about to be slaughtered, sniffing and prancing between our ankles. Then we load ourselves back into the Kangoo and head down toward the highway.

But the road that led up from the highway somehow does not lead back to the highway. We wander a maze of streets then stop to try and get our bearings. Far above and in front of us, cutting across the high hillsides, is a winding Interstate perched precariously on hundred-foot-tall concrete stilts. My mother, who doesn't like heights at all, says, "I'm glad we're not going that way, at least."

We see a mother and daughter approaching, and ask them how to get to the road to Isernia. They point up to the highway on stilts.

"Sorry Mum," I say over my shoulder.

"It's okay."

We find the exit from the town and climb and climb, crossing windswept stretches of highway perched a thousand feet above one of Abruzzo's stony valleys. Buffeted by the strong gusts, the trucks in front of us waver and tilt. Something is wrong. I smell something I shouldn't be smelling. For a few miles I wonder if one of the trucks is burning oil, or if what I'm smelling is our clutch, truly destroyed now, in which case we will have to glide down out of the mountains on this road on stilts, in the wind, the Kangoo half out of control, the trucks tilting, the girls screaming, the man behind the wheel wrapped in a desperate struggle with nausea, with an evil mood . . . Something smells very strongly and badly. I wonder if Juliana might need another diaper change so soon. But no, this is something else. In a very strained version of the Happy Dad voice I say: "Check your shoes, everybody."

Everybody checks their shoes. We have reached the summit of this mountain range now and are overlooking the city of Castel di Sangro. The smell has grown stronger. With all but one of the precincts reporting, there are no bottom-of-the-shoe-problems. High up on a windswept rise, I pull over into a turnoff that is strewn with every imaginable size, shape, and type of paper, plastic, and metal litter. I check my boots. I curse. I step out, cursing, in the cold wind, find a small piece of plastic, and go to work. These are new boots, bought specially for this trip. Their hard soles have countless little channels in them, deep but narrow channels meant to give traction on snowy driveways and muddy hiking trails, but filled now with the fresh droppings of one or more of the Abruzzo's friendly dogs. I hear noises from the car, through the windows. These are not good noises. Trucks rumble past a few feet away. My back hurts. I have the flu now, surely. I am working away at my odious task with the piece of plastic and some paper. Five minutes. Ten minutes. It's an impossible job; the new hiking boots will have to be soaked in bleach, soaked in acid, thrown out. I toss the paper aside into the pile of litter. The passengers are restless, the boots only half-clean. I scuff them furiously in the dust and gravel, furiously, furiously, toss the plastic into the wind, and climb back in behind the wheel.

"It's a sign from God," I say, not very nicely. "It's some kind of curse."

"What is, Dad?" Alexandra asks.

And I say: "Nothing, honey."

15

Here's the problem: on our map, the road south of Avezzano, Highway 17, looks fairly straight. It is important to find a straight road without too many mountain curves for several reasons: One, my mother is uncomfortable with heights, as I've mentioned, and she has put up with enough as it is and I want to spare her the personal terror of looking out the side window and down a two-thousand foot drop. Two, as I did when I was a child, Alexandra gets carsick easily on winding roads. Three, we are still concerned about Juliana and want the road that will be least likely to make her vomit. Four, I feel very much like vomiting.

So, south of Castel de Sangro, Highway 17, which looks more or less straight on our map, turns out to be precisely the road from hell.

We see a sign that says ISERNIA 36. Thirty-six kilometers is about twenty-two miles. No problem. I could do twenty-two miles in my sleep, with the flu, with mongrel feces in the hard channels of my new boots, with a curtain of regret draped over me from head to toe, with the kids arguing in back and a creeping nausea working its way up my sternum. Thirty-six kilometers is nothing. Not a problem.

What the sign does not say is that there are more switchback turns on the road to Isernia than on any other road on earth. We glide down two hundred yards, make a switchback hairpin turn to the left. A hundred more yards, a switchback hairpin turn to the right. "I'm feeling real bad," Alexandra says. Amanda turns around to check on her, and then on Juliana, and tells me that the younger of our girls has that look on her face again. My mother is utterly silent. Another switchback turn, another, another, another, another, a truck coming the other way, wheels in our lane. It's like skiing a black diamond trail with the stomach flu, holding a young child on each shoulder. In order to make things a little easier, I start cutting the corners, gliding into the opposite lane even though doing this means I can't quite see trucks that might be coming the other way. Straightening the road a bit, Italian-style. Another switchback, another, another, another, another, another.

This goes on, unbelievably, for the better part of an hour. Amanda is getting dizzy, can't look at the map. "This reminds me of that road we took in the fog in France," she says. We had just crossed over from Italy and were winding down out of the Alps as darkness fell, passing small cliffs with a river twisting below. Each new loop and curve brought another striking scene into view. A few men were fly-fishing in the river, I remember that; and I remember thinking it was some of the finest scenery I'd ever encountered—the craggy rock faces with trees sprouting from crevices and standing guard on top, the twirling river, the sense that we had stumbled into secret territory known only to painters from a century long passed. But then the light was gone, and a soupy fog descended over those valleys, and soon we could see only a few car lengths in front of us. The road wound almost in curlicues, rising and dipping through dark little stone villages. Both of us grew so car sick that we had to pull over in one of the villages and walk around for a while, looking in vain for an open store where we might buy a few crackers or some soda.

Everyone is as woozy as that, now, on the road to Isernia,

but there is no place to stop. The interior of the Kangoo shifts and spins like a below-decks cabin in a storm.

This goes on and on and on, an endless spinning torment. It seems impossible that any road could be built this way. Why even bother? Why not just route everyone around the base of whatever mountain range we're crossing, rather than put them through this?

But at last the road straightens, and we make a quick, steady descent into Isernia. At this point Juliana has another attack of diarrhea. We stop in a bar and Amanda takes her into the bathroom and changes her. While I'm waiting in the bar we order coffee and Cokes and brioches for the whole nauseous, dizzy, tired, uncomplaining bunch of us and I strike up a conversation with a truck driver. "We're going to Lecce," I tell him. "But I want to take the road that has the fewest curves on it. Nothing else matters. Even if we have to go a hundred miles out of our way, I want a straight road."

"Go to Vasto," he says immediately. "To Vasto the road is very straight."

The road to Vasto, Highway 650 according to our excellent map, will bring us somewhat northward, but to the coast. Amanda wants to keep moving south; the drive is long enough as it is, why make it longer? But I vote for Vasto and mount a persuasive argument. For one thing, the truck driver promised that there are few curves. For another, since Vasto is on the water, I believe there will be an *agriturismo* there, nice beds, great food. I have a sense about these things, I tell Amanda, and, after a minute or two she says, "All right, let's try it."

Vasto, I will write, a few days later, in my notes. *Vasto this.*

16

The road to Vasto is, in fact, a fairly straight one, and quite picturesque. We are in the province of Molise now, a kidney-shaped cut of Italian landscape lodged between the central mountains and the Adriatic coast. According to one of our guide books, bears, wolves and wild boar live on this land. The hills are dry and brown, but set in dusty opposition to each other in such a way that they suggest a long history of human occupation and human use. I love land like this. Even with a thin fever creeping across the terrain of my skin, I love it. A river with a gravelly bed—the Trigno—winds along beside the highway, crossing beneath us now, spilling past gravel beaches then curling back against steep dirt banks. There are vineyards in the shadows. On the long downhill slope, mottled with tunnels, we have to make one emergency stop ("I think she has a poop, Mom.") I will not go into the details of this poop except to say that Amanda, who never litters, ever, anywhere, takes the diaper when we're finished, wraps it into a tight smelly bundle, and, without saying a word, walks over to a six-foot-high wall at the side of the rest area and flings the diaper over so that it mingles with half a ton or so of other garbage. Vasto.

We reach Vasto, or the outskirts of Vasto, close to sundown, and head south along the coast. The pale water of the Adriatic, tropical blue here, laps at a shore not a hundred yards to our left, and the area seems blessed, warm, sunny. Any minute now, any minute, there will be a sign for an *agriturismo*

But there isn't. We pass through the crowded seaside city of Termoli, timing it perfectly so we arrive during rush hour. We stop there in a real estate office and ask about lodging, but the agent is of no help. As I am negotiating a difficult, crowded rotary just past the city, trying to stay alert in the soup of aggressive drivers, Juliana vomits again. I shoot over to the side of the road, cutting across three lanes of traffic and we stop there beneath an overpass, cars and trucks whizzing past, drivers honking, waving their arms, sneering, smiling in admiration. Amanda and I lean over with towels and do our best to mop up.

I will not go into the details here, of the hour that follows. Darkness is falling, I will say that. I will say, too, that Amanda and I argue, but I will not go into the details of that argument because it is too painful to remember.

I will say that the children are hungry, that Juliana has the miserable and frightening dulled look on her face, that I feel as if I've put my head and body into a *machina per la bucca* and drunk deeply of the gray wash water there and then let the machine spin me around and around for a full day. At one point in this hour, I go into a gas station bar and ask a couple of characters where the nearest hotel might be. "There, right here," one of them says. "You can walk to it." I do walk to it. The hotel, right beside this gas station, is closed for the season, so either the guys in the garage work right beside it and don't know it's closed, or they know and are playing a little game to pass the winter evening. Ha, there's another frazzled American with his family, asking directions. The kids look sick, too. Ha. Let's do the one about the hotel right next door and see how he reacts.

In fact, all the hotels along this gorgeous dark coast are closed. Sometimes they are closed but leave the sign on: H O T

118

E L, so that Amanda keeps pointing them out to me. And I keep snapping back that they are closed, closed, don't you understand?

At last, we find a hotel that seems to be open. It is decided that I should go in and inquire. After I've been standing in the reception area for two minutes, a somewhat wobbly elderly man who hasn't shaved in two days drags himself away from a soccer game on the TV in the breakfast nook and looks at me as if I am a figure from a particular sexual fantasy he has been nurturing in the most secret recesses of his brain for the last half century. In spite of this, I ask about rooms. "I'll have to call the *signora*," he says.

"Fine," I say, not very nicely. "Call her then."

He looks at me for an unconscionably long time, thirty or forty seconds. It is as if I'm watching a movie of him and the screen has frozen. Then he goes back to his soccer game. I stand by the desk. I should say here, again, that I am not a violent person, not at all. But the truth is that, as the *signora's* arrival is delayed and delayed, and the older soccer fan shows no inclination to let her know of the presence of a paying customer, I am in a mood to go behind the desk and take the cappuccino machine there and smash it and smash it, and . . . the man returns. He stands there staring at me. I'm on the verge of walking out. "What are we waiting for?" I demand.

He looks at me for a few seconds without speaking, and then says, *"La signora."*

When the *signora* comes, she is a very nice *signora*, a woman of such good will, such gentleness, such southern Italian grace that I am ashamed of myself for my thoughts, my outbursts, the vitriol that lives deep deep in me and can be raised to the surface by something as simple as a sign reading H O T E L and a good wife mentioning it. In fact, it was Juliana getting sick again that tipped the scales. I am normally a patient and

119

good tempered man, a calm father, a considerate husband. Given the state of my health, I would like to make the claim here that I had dealt with things fairly well that day—cleaning dog excrement from my boots in the cold I'd barely said a word that would be censored these days on AM radio. But the thought that Juliana might be truly ill, that the doctors in Rome missed something, that we had dragged her four hundred miles south, away from the best medical care in the country . . . that is the thing that breaks my composure open and spills the bitterness out into the air around me.

But just the presence of this woman sets me straight. She takes me upstairs in the elevator (the only elevator I have ever seen that is lacking two walls. As we rise, the concrete blocks of the building pass by a few feet from our bodies on either side. "Careful," she says.) But the rooms are clean and pleasant looking, and the price is not unreasonable (120 Euros for both rooms, including breakfast; a little over 130 dollars at the current exchange) considering the fact that this seems to be the only open hotel along this coast for fifty miles in either direction.

And, though, alas, there is no restaurant on the premises, the graceful *signora* is kind enough to provide directions to a place to eat in the nearby town, Campomarino: Out the gate, right, right again at the intersection, and then, of course, *sempre diritto*. One kilometer. You can't possibly miss it. We are back in the lobby now, and I've put another charge on our overburdened credit card. I ask her to repeat the directions, and the old man takes his eyes from the soccer game and gives me another long look.

We back the Kangoo carefully out of the hotel lot, turn right, right again, and immediately get lost in a grid of seaside streets lined with palm trees and empty dark houses. I gnash and mutter and make an illegal U-turn. We go back to the hotel and start over again, with one small change, and this time we find our way out of the maze, and down another street, that leads, not to the *signora's* restaurant, but at least to a seaside boulevard, on which there seems to be one lighted commercial establishment. We stop near it, but, having had some experience with such places in my youth, I see that it is a raucous bar, not suitable for children and ill adults. The Queen of Optimism, however, my patient and wonderful queen, thinks it might work as a dinner destination. "Go ahead and take a look, then, if you think it might work," I say. SNAP! She gets out of the car, walks halfway to the bar and turns around. "No," she says. "It won't work."

"Alright. Sorry."

We go back to the intersection near the hotel, try another road that approximately matches the directions, and there, probably just where the *signora* promised it would be, we find the restaurant. Turn off the Kangoo, unfasten the seatbelts, lift Juliana out, help Alexandra out, help Ma out, carry a small assortment of books and games to keep the girls busy, go inside. We are hungry, our hopes are high. The restaurant is very cold. Someone, several people, are smoking, and a tobacco fog swirls above the tables. The owner tells us that, alas, unfortunately, they do not have a machine for the credit cards; as always, we are not carrying enough cash.

We go back outside. We can smell the ocean in the damp air. In a sort of strip mall across the street we see another restaurant, and it turns out that this establishment does take credit cards, and that it is presided over by a man who looks exactly like John Travolta. Not just a little bit like John Travolta, *exactly* like him. Speaking nearly perfect English, he shows us to a table, and then begins to go into great detail about the seafood specialties he offers. Swordfish. Prawns. Crabs. Mussels. And how they are prepared, with what spices, and so on.

"We just want pasta," I say. "Simple pasta for the girls. And a mussels appetizer for me, then *pasta basilica*."

My mother cautions me about the mussels, but I am not in the mood to be cautious. The worse I feel, the more I want something delicious on a plate in front of me. Unsteady on my feet, I accompany Alexandra to the bathroom.

In a few minutes a pretty waitress brings the mussels, which are superb. Another little while and the pasta arrives. Then the owner serves me the single best glass of red wine I have ever drunk in my life, "made from grapes that grow right near here," he says proudly. "A kilometer away." This wine is enough to make you stop making fun of the vocabulary of oenophiles, forever. It bursts against the palate with subtle hints of cherry and plum, a touch of spice, a smooth strong middle range, and then a fine long leathery finish with sparkles of . . . When I compliment the owner on this vintage, he pours the rest of the bottle into my glass, no charge. I feel like throwing up. I feel like dying. But nothing, nothing could keep me from finishing this glass of wine. I eat all the mussels while Ma watches me closely. She and the girls and Amanda give a thumbs-up for their food. I eat a few bites of the pasta, and get up out of my chair to ask a man who comes in after us if he would please put out his cigarette because my daughter has a respiratory illness. I have to switch to English to get this last part out. He is amazingly gracious about it. "What respiratory illness?" Alexandra asks when I sit down again. "I don't have any respiratory illness."

Afterwards, while the women are checking to see if the toilet has a seat, I go up to the counter to pay John Travolta, and I tell him, quietly, that I would like to buy the man at that table a grappa. I explain that our oldest daughter has cystic fibrosis, and that I'd asked him to put out his cigarette because tobacco smoke is especially unhealthy for her, and that he was very decent about it. John Travolta says: "If you had told me that, I would have gone around myself and made everyone stop smoking."

This, I think, waiting for my loved ones in a cold parking lot, this is why you come back to Italy, this grace, this big-heartedness, this nice end to one of the worst days of your life.

17

Nausea is a kind of lesser cousin to the truly bad things a body is capable of doing to itself. I have known some serious and protracted pain in my life—a bad case of shingles, a broken back, terrible arthritis flare-ups—but nausea is somehow worse. I spend the entire night in Campomarino on the edge of vomiting. From time to time, Juliana wakes up screaming in the crib beside the bed. Amanda gets up to soothe her. I lie there, burping, tossing back and forth, a skewered man.

In the morning, I have two bites of breakfast, and we head out, down the coast, stopping once to sample the dense, honking traffic in the dusty city of Foggia, and to change Travelers Cheques there and get some cash.

Miserable though I am, I console myself with dreams of Lecce. The rest of the crew seems to have weathered the storm.

At least there's no danger of curving roads here because we've left the mountainous middle of Italy behind. We are riding down the Adriatic coast, the calf of the boot, heading toward the heel. This arid land, occupied by a series of invaders—Greek, Roman, Norman, Spanish— is mostly flat, lit by a semi-tropical sun, with olive groves by the road, and butter-yellow flowers in bloom beneath old, gnarled, heat-shortened trees, cactus sprouting here and there beyond the guardrails, and a kind of bird we haven't seen, perched on the fence posts, crow-sized, gray tail twitching.

Juliana seems to be feeling better. I am feeling worse. Still, I love to eat, and love to see people around me enjoying a meal, so when, on the outskirts of the resort town of Monopoli, we see an advertisement for an Indian restaurant, I become excited. The clouds of nausea lift momentarily. It goes without saying that Italian cuisine is wonderful, but, in the restaurants at least, it can be a bit monotonous: salad, pasta, a cut of veal (which I don't eat) or beef. For people like us—people spoiled by being able to have a Chinese meal now and then, or a Thai meal, a burrito, sushi, baklava—even in the culinary miracle that is Italy we sometimes experience a twinge of longing for more variety.

We especially love Indian food. At home, Alexandra votes Indian every time we're trying to decide where to go for a meal out. She loves *raita*, she loves *naan*, she loves tandoori chicken; we all do. And so, when we see the billboard outside Monopoli, a thrill runs through the air of the car. There is some stop-and-go traffic on the dusty road, more signs advertising this place. At last, we see the restaurant itself. We park across the street, prepare to get out. "It looks closed," Amanda says. I stagger across the road and try the door. *Chiuso*.

Farther down the beach road we see signs for another restaurant, take the turn indicated, and find ourselves in a dead-end parking lot on the water. More graffiti here, a young couple sitting on the wall, making out in enthusiastic, R-rated fashion. The windows of the buildings are shuttered, there is no restaurant in view, and the sun is shining brightly off a pastel sea. We drive back to the highway and head south for forty-five minutes, come into another little town, and follow more signs to another restaurant, right on the water. Out front there is a sign that says APERTO but the place is obviously closed. We turn around and are heading back toward the main road when we see a fellow on the street corner opposite us. It would be difficult, perhaps impossible, *not* to see this fellow. He is madly waving his arms and smiling as if he is the brother or uncle we've come all these thousands of miles to find. We pull over and he hurries up to the Kangoo. On his face is an expression you see on the faces of con-artists the world over—a horrible mix of desperation, false camaraderie, a certain shining central ray of attention in the midst of a small universe of attention deficit. "It's open, it's open, of course my restaurant is open!" he sings out. He is leaning on the car with both hands now, his face close to mine. "Are you hungry? *Avete fame?*" He leans in toward the girls and switches to English: "Do you want eat? Do you want eat here?"—he gestures to the little corner store from which he seems to have emerged—"or there?"—he waves his right arm at the "open" restaurant, a couple hundred yards away on the water's edge.

"*Vicino al mare,*" I say. "Near the water,"

"*Vicino al mare, bene!* Near the water, fine! Just drive down there, then. Drive down! My sister cooks! We will be right there! We will meet you!"

"Seems like a nice man," Amanda says.

I mutter something under my breath, the polite equivalent of which might be "con-artist", but I am too weary, too sick, too broken-hearted to put up an argument. I drive the Kangoo down, park it in front of the restaurant, and all of us get out. I forget to put on the emergency brake, and the Kangoo starts to roll in the direction of the ocean, which splashes and churns just beyond a steep drop-off, ten meters away. I jump in and hit the brake. One measure of my mental state is this: It occurs to me, mid-jump, that maybe it wouldn't be such a bad thing to let the car coast right into the sea.

"Do you take credit cards?" I ask the man, when that almost-emergency has been taken care of. He has flown down to meet us, sister in tow.

I'm hoping he will say no, because I simply do not like him. But he says: "Of course, of course. *Si, si, certo!*"

It's windy and cool near the water, but the sun is shining, and the sea, a translucent blue/green, is splashing happily against a shoreline of coral boulders. I ask if we might eat inside, near a window, but unfortunately, sad to say, sorry for the inconvenience, although the restaurant is in fact open, the inside is locked. There is one other party of six eating on the windy patio and I hear a few words of English being spoken there.

In fact, as it turns out, the sister will have to do the cooking back up at the corner store and carry the food down to us. No one but the Americans seems to be made uncomfortable by this. A plastic table is set up outside the patio, out of the wind. There's no menu, but they will be happy to prepare us some pasta, and the specialty of the house, fresh fried octopus. "We'll pass on the octopus," I say, quite clearly, the man nodding, the sister looking tired. "Just some pasta, bread, water, a salad we can share. Do you have Coca Cola?"

"*Bene, bene. Certo!*" the fellow says. "Wonderful, fine. Of course!"

While we wait for the food to be prepared, Alexandra and my mother wander off to check out the ocean. Amanda takes the baby someplace and changes her diaper, announcing, when she returns, that there has been an improvement in consistency. Dad sits in the plastic chair with head in hands, in the sun, in the cool breeze, and concentrates on the feelings in his stomach. In a little while the sister appears with someone who may be the con-artist's wife, carrying trays of pasta, bread, and bottled mineral water. We are also served a large bottle of Coke, special treat for girls brought up on water, milk and juice. We eat. Another few minutes, and the second course is

carried down: a heaping plate of fried octopus. "We didn't order   these," Amanda starts to say, but what's the use?

"If the baby isn't feeling well," the man trumpets, "this is
exactly the thing for her!"

There isn't one chance in twenty million that Juliana will eat
the octopus, but I've had octopus before, and these look fresh
and delicious, lightly battered and fried up crisp. So against my
better judgment (and my mother's: she is shaking her head at
me from the end of the table. "Rol," she says, "If you have an
upset stomach I don't think octopus is a very good idea . . .). I
try some. Wonderful. I try some more. I eat five or six of them
and ask for the rest to be packed up.

The restaurateur is at the side of the table, shining his oversized smile on us like four suns. We order dessert for Alexandra and my mother. He's there again, glistening, almost bow-
ing, thrilled beyond description. "We don't know how much it's
going to cost," Amanda quietly reminds me. But the man presents us with the bill and it is reasonable. Thirty Euros. I nod,
compliment him on the octopus, take out my credit card and
hold it toward him.

And he says: "I'm sorry, forgive me. *Scusi.* But we don't
take credit cards."

<u>18</u>

Now our kamikaze dive into southernmost Italy is coming to an end; we are zeroing in on the city of Lecce. We pass the hideous outskirts of Brindisi, all oil refineries, abandoned cars, and enormous blocks of tattered apartment complexes. "It gets to be over a hundred here in the summer," I say, perhaps because of my fever. "Imagine what it's like to sleep in one of those places on an August night."

The ferry from Greece stops here. And this is the place where, periodically, a boat overflowing with Albanian refugees will drift ashore, the passengers hungry, thirsty, and sea-sick, having fled a country driven to desperate poverty by the communist version of corruption and power-madness. To these refugees, I imagine, Brindisi looks like a dusty painting from the museums of heaven. To us it does not.

We race on, the highway arrow-straight now, the weather sunnier, maybe a few degrees warmer. I smell my fried octopus, cooking a second time there near the back window, in the heat.

At last, we make it into the outer edge of Lecce, and call our contact, whose name is Stefano, from a payphone near the front door of the best hotel in town. This hotel has well-groomed clerks behind gleaming granite counters, a beautiful swimming pool, foreign periodicals in the lobby. But, alas, I am informed by my sources, no paper in the women's toilets.

"There were seats, at least, right?" I ask them, and I'm answered by a trio of nods.

Stefano soon appears. He steps out of his car in sunglasses, looking dapper, young, sane, healthy—all the things I am not. "How has your vacation been?" he inquires in lightly accented English.

"Fine," I say. "Wonderful so far."

He looks away while we change the baby's diaper on the hood of the car (no place to do this in the paperless bathrooms), and then he leads us into the heart of the city. Or, almost into the heart of the city. "Unfortunately," he says, when we park near one of the gates to the Florence of the South, "we don't yet have the pass for your automobile, and the apartment is in the pedestrian zone, so you'll have to leave your car here just for tonight. The apartment itself is only a hundred meters from here."

An Italian hundred meters.

I happen to know what a hundred meters is. It so happens that, on a good day, I can hit a golf ball, with my gap wedge, exactly a hundred and ten yards, or a hundred meters. The apartment is more like half a mile from where we park. Which, under normal circumstances, would not matter at all, but on this sunny late afternoon in Lecce I feel like I can walk about twenty feet.

The wheels of the stroller clatter on the cobbled pavement and we soon notice that there are quite a number of cars in the pedestrian zone. The streets have no sidewalks. But though "Florence of the South" seems somewhat of an exaggeration, the city is pretty and welcoming, with three-story sandstone buildings pressed shoulder-to-shoulder, many of them decorated with carved gargoyles and fronted with balconies and wrought-iron railings.

We complete the half mile, then turn right, off the winding, cobbled, busy main thoroughfare into a sort of half-courtyard, half-alley. Stefano stops in front of the second entrance on the left and leads us through a five-foot-high wooden door. We climb two flights of stairs to what turns out to be an absolutely palatial apartment. There are two bedrooms, one so enormous that the *matrimonionale* looks like a matchbox with a scrap of white cloth covering the mattress. A large, almost empty living room, large dining room, small kitchen with tiled counters, two baths. It must be close to a thousand square feet, half the size of our house in America. The ceilings are vaulted, sixteen feet high, and decorated with old faded frescoes and fresh detailing, the walls painted in shades of soft gray and salmon.

It's clean and beautiful, miraculous, a gift from the travel gods.

No one but me seems to like it.

I have no appetite, none. My body, it seems, is unwilling to digest the fried octopus we had for lunch. Imagine what it feels like to have no appetite in Italy, to be surrounded by stores selling two-dollar bottles of excellent red wine, fresh tomatoes and resplendent cheeses, just-cooked bread and rolls and cakes; bars where you can stand up and have a ninety-cent macchiato or a fresh-squeezed blood orange juice; restaurants where there are long tables covered with warm plates of grilled peppers and eggplant, green beans in garlic, soft balls of mozzarella, sardines and anchovies, meatballs and sausages; where the menus offer three dozen kinds of pizza, or twenty kinds of pasta . . . and not be hungry. This, it seems to me, is the definition of illness.

Amanda stays behind to change Juliana. I need air. Stefano, my mother, Alexandra, and I descend the long narrow flights of stairs, step out through the neck-high door and into the courtyard.

There, Stefano introduces us to Giorgio, the owner of the

131

apartment, who is an orthodontist and who has just driven up and popped out of his new Mercedes convertible. From behind designer sunglasses and a dazzling smile, Giorgio asks how I like the apartment and I say that I like it very much. "My wife is always going to Cortina D'Ampezzo," he says, pronouncing the name of the glitzy ski resort in the Dolomites with some disdain. "There, apartments like this go for three or four times what we are charging you."

I maintain eye contact with him as well as I can through the sunglasses and the shimmering fields of nausea playing near my forehead. I try, without words, to convey the impression that, at this particular moment, I could not possibly care less what this apartment would rent for in Cortina D'Ampezzo. It is Lecce. It is the off-season. The apartment is, in fact, magnificent, but it's not like there were thousands of other prospective renters lined up in the pedestrian zone ready to move in. Giorgio smiles, an advertisement. In order to say something other than what I'm thinking, I tell him I am looking forward to playing golf, though, at the moment, I could no more play a single hole of golf than I could fly up and over the stuccoed buildings of Via Palmieri and all the way to the slopes of Cortina D'Ampezzo. "How is the course here?"

Giorgio makes his face into the classic Italian expression of pity, pressing his lips out and down, raising his eyebrows a quarter of an inch, casting his eyes to one side. "*Piccolo*" he says. Little. Unimpressive. Pitiable. "If you are used to real courses, this one will be" . . . he makes a dismissive gesture. "*Piccolo*."

After another few pleasantries—Giorgio is an affable, impatient sort—he shoots off in his Mercedes. Stefano makes sure we have his cell phone number and strides off toward his car. Two young neighborhood boys appear, Alessandro and Lucca, thrilled to learn we are from America. We stand and talk with them for a few minutes. While we wait for Amanda to finish changing Juliana's diaper, my mother, Alexandra, and, to a certain extent, Alexandra's sick dad, kick the soccer ball back and forth with the boys in the open courtyard. At one point, Alessandro, a wonderfully feisty little kid with a promising future as a juvenile delinquent, asks me what my wife's name is. He is pointing to my mother. "That's my mother," I say. "She's Eileen. She's eighty."

"Eighty?" he says, as if I must not know my Italian numbers. "*Ottanta?*"

"Si." I watch his eyes as they run over my mother's face, her hair, her trim body.

"Eighty," he says. "And she kicks a soccer ball?"

Another few kicks and passes and then, just for fun, Alessandro drills a hard shot against the neighbor's beautifully lacquered green front door, once, twice. Bangs one up near her windows. In a moment she opens the door, steps out and says, "How many times do I have to tell you!" etcetera, etcetera. Which is what aggrieved homeowners say the world over to kids like Alessandro, kids like me. He hangs his head and looks away, with a devilish little grin trying to catch the corners of his lips, and I am cast back to a quiet block crowded with houses in the Massachusetts city where I was raised. I and my friends—Frankie and Johnny Imbrescia, Albert Santosuosso, Jimmy Giberti, Johnny Verengia, Carmine Luongo, Michael Capone—all of us of Italian descent, are playing a game of touch football in the street in front of my house, tossing errant passes into the neighbors' flower gardens, kicking punts that bounce once on the roof of someone's Chevy, ricochet off aluminum siding, tear a piece off a shrub and go wobbling down into the Famigliettis' trash cans where they make a loud bang. It was as if, like Alessandro, we were young socialist revolutionaries at play, claiming all property as our own.

Amanda steps out through the small wooden door, carrying Juliana under one arm, the diaper bag over one shoulder, and looking reasonably pleased about the consistency of things.

"The course is *piccolo*," I tell her, but this information isn't the kind of crushing blow I expect it to be.

Amanda and the girls are hungry and want to go out looking for supper. I volunteer to make a couple of trips to the car and bring in the rest of our baggage.

"But you can hardly stand up," Amanda says.

I shrug it off. I must go on, must make my penance, my amends. While the rest of the gang hunts for a meal in the cool darkness of the Florence of the South, I drag myself step by gruesome step along Via Palmieri toward the car, wondering all the way if there might be a bathroom close by. Acquaintances of ours, an American couple, once left their car, full of luggage, along the side of a southern Italian road while they went for a leisurely bicycle ride. When they returned from the ride a few hours later, the car had been cleaned out. Mimmo told us it was "a country of thieves". And an expatriate Englishman we met at the octopus restaurant said, "It's nice here; just watch your wallet."

Amanda and I had our rented car broken into once in southern France in the middle of the night. The thief very carefully and neatly removed the rubber that held the rear passenger-side window in place, removed my new winter coat from the back seat, carefully emptied the pockets and left the contents in the car, carefully set the window down against the tire. Once, not far from Boston, while Amanda and I were swimming, someone threw a stone through the passenger side window of our car and stole my jeans, wallet, license, credit cards, and a hundred and thirty dollars in cash.

So all these bits of our history are rattling around in my thoughts as I make the grim march along Via Palmieri. I am worried about the golf clubs, mostly. My Hogans. My sticks.

Beyond the Porta Napoli, outside the city wall, the night sky is darker, the parking area poorly lit. I see a man lounging around there, dressed in shabby clothes, with a cigarette hanging out of one side of his mouth. From the pocket of his tattered jacket this man takes a cell phone and speaks into it in a conspiratorial tone, the tone of a criminal, the tone of a thief, or worse. I square my shoulders, make myself—at six feet, a hundred and seventy-five pounds—look as big and rough as I possibly can. I open the back of the Kangoo, take the golf bag out, take out my computer, slam the door closed and conspicuously beep the door locks. I look straight at the man. He looks straight at me. We say nothing. Step by awful step I start back up Via Palmieri toward the palace we will be living in for the next eight nights. Sweating, breathing hard, burping every few seconds, completely without energy, I make it to our little alley, stoop through the green door, leave the golf bag in the entranceway, and carry my computer up the forty-six narrow steps that lead to our new place of residence. I rest there, arms stiff on a windowsill, until my head clears a bit, then make a second trip to the Kangoo.

The man is still lurking there in the shadows, studying the line of cars like the professional thief I know him to be. I imagine him calling his boss on the cell phone, saying: "He's back, the American. They have a ton of stuff in there, he can't possibly carry it all. I'm thinking he's going to leave something in the car and forget to lock the back door. The second he's gone, I'm in there."

He approaches me across the dark lot. He has one hand in a jacket pocket. I turn from the car and face him. When we're four feet apart he says: "I'm on duty only until eleven o'clock." As though he is hinting for a tip.

I say: "*Bene*". Good. I consider giving him the little white paper bag with my fried octopus in it, practically fermented now from sitting in the heat and sun. I fish the last couple of bags out of the Kangoo and start back.

It turns out, when the gang returns to the apartment, that all of the restaurants in this part of Lecce are closed. "Of course they're all closed," I say bitterly. "Why wouldn't they be closed? Why should a restaurant be open?"

"They open at eight o'clock, Dad," Alexandra says patiently. "People eat dinner later in Italy."

19

I spend a miserable night in the palatial bedroom, listening to Amanda breathe evenly in her sleep, and Juliana toss and turn in the portable crib a few feet away. I'm feverish, twitching, aching, and something so terrible is transpiring in my intestines that every hour or so I have to force myself to get up and stagger into the bathroom. The young woman in the Contigliano library had said it affects adults only for one day. One day, I keep telling myself. One bad day. To keep a degree of mental stability, I play imaginary golf games at courses I remember back home. Edge Hill. Worthington. Red Tail. Taconic. Crumpin Fox.

At two-thirty a.m. just after my fourth toilet run, I hear a terrible noise in the other bedroom, then a scream. The noise is the sound of Alexandra's skull hitting the stone floor. I yell out, too, a kind of empathy-reflex, waking everyone who is not already awake. Amanda and I go in and comfort Alexandra, who will walk around for the next week with an egg-shaped lump on her forehead.

In bed again, I say to Amanda, "I think there's some bad energy surrounding this vacation. I think it's cursed." In a few more seconds she's asleep.

20

But the Florence of the South turns out to be an improvement over just about everything we have seen so far on our fabulous Italian vacation. Suffering from my one-day flu, I spend the better part of the first three days in Lecce either lying in bed, hurrying to the bathroom, or slumped in a chair at the dining room table, watching Amanda, my mother, and the girls eat. Juliana is almost back to normal, we are all grateful for that. And no one else seems to have been afflicted.

Slowly, hour by bad hour over the course of three days, the flu releases its grip on me. When I am well enough to stand up and get dressed, I shuffle once around the block and see that the streets of Lecce are lined with pretty shops, and that there are two impressive Norman churches close by, and that the place has a unique charm to it—not like Florence at all, but attractive in an understated, sand-brown way. After an initial cool spell, the weather has warmed into the fifties.

More important than anything else—than Norman cathedrals or magnificent works of art or friendly people or good golf—there is a playground near the center of the Florence of the South. And so, when I am finally able to drag myself out of bed and take a shower, when I feel ready to rejoin the world in a serious way, my mother and I take the girls to the playground. Amanda needs a day off. From the start of this trip she's been cooking meals, shopping, lifting Juliana into and out

TAKING THE KIDS TO ITALY

of her car seat, changing her, soothing her in the middle of the night. I help as much as I can with these duties, and my mother is a tremendous help, but for the last few days I've been out of commission, and Amanda has been doing the work of two. She gave up a promising photography career to be a full-time mother, and she misses the work, I know. On this warm Monday I tell her to grab her camera bag and wander around the city for a few hours. My mother and I will take the girls. The weather is decent. There's a playground. She says, "Are you sure you're feeling up to it?" But I can see the look of relief on her face.

For a few minutes after Amanda takes leave of us, lugging her thirty-pound camera bag, Juliana will not stop crying. "Mama! MAMA!" she yells. "MAMA! . . . ME! . . . GO!"

"Playground," I say. "Slide."

"NO. MAMA! NO!"

Alexandra hugs her and talks to her. I ply her with a soft roll and some digestive crackers. In time, she calms down. I get her shoes and coat on, carry her down the forty-six steps and place her in the stroller, and Alexandra and my mother accompany us through the sidewalkless streets of Lecce, hugging close to the old stone housefronts whenever a car scurries past.

The playground is set a quarter mile or so from the historical center, in a good-sized park with a snack shop and a pretty, green-roofed gazebo. There are two playgrounds there, in fact, two small gravel areas with plastic slides, wooden climbing structures, and swings. You have to cross a busy street to get there, however, and the drivers don't like stop for you. (Eventually, after watching an Italian family navigate this busy street that borders the playground, I learn the proper technique: you wait for a tiny gap in the three lanes of traffic, then march out into it, putting your body between the oncoming vehicles and your children. You hold out one stiff arm with your palm facing the drivers, look sternly into their faces, make them feel as guilty as possible for endangering the lives of *i bambini*, and, usually, they stop.)

A playground is, for Alexandra and Juliana, what a golf course is for me and my mother, what a day walking a foreign city with her camera is for Amanda. Just the sight, just the idea of it, just the word brings a happy light to their faces. Alexandra climbs on everything, runs up the slides the wrong way even though we tell her not to, swings on the swings, rides in the swinging carriages, runs, jumps, her overjoyed voice echoing back toward the center of town. Juliana wants to go on the slides, period. If there are four slides, she wants to go on all four of them. "Me. Up," she says, and I lift her to the top of the slide, set her down there, make sure she's lined up straight, and say, "Ready, set, go!" She looks at me, says, "Ray, zett, goh!" and the expression on her face as she zips down toward a gravel landing—well, for me, that expression more than compensates for three very bad nights spent burping in bed.

We pass the better part of an hour there, scolded, eventually, by the sort-of policeman whose job it is to maintain order. His is an especially difficult job because kids between the ages of one and five have been known to start revolutions in other parts of the world, to commit atrocities, to do irreparable damage to unbreakable plastic climbing structures. So the sort-of policeman is very strict with us. At one point, Juliana does the unforgivable: she tosses a few handfuls of gravel on the bottom of the slide because she likes to hear the sound it makes against the red plastic. There are no other children around, and Dad will always sweep off the gravel when she's through, so this little stunt endangers no one. But the sort-of policeman has an eye and an ear for these types of treacheries, and he hurries over, yelling at me that my daughter is committing a breach of the park rules. A breach of the park rules, stop her. Stop her!

I pretend not to hear at first, not to notice him, and then, not to understand. I make him say whatever he's saying twice, three times, four times. I let his blood pressure rise. And then I sweep the gravel off the slide with one swipe of my arm, lift Juliana up, and soothe both girls by promising them that rarest of treats in our family: lunch at McDonald's.

Before lunch, though, we need to get some cash. Experienced travelers that we are, Amanda and I loaded up on Travelers Cheques before leaving home, and we keep only a small amount of cash on us. This is actually a stupid thing to do, but we've been doing it all our traveling lives and the stupidity of it, in this particular situation, has yet to dawn on us. Not far from the playground, I see a branch of the same bank we used in Rieti—out of kindness I will not print the name of the bank here—so I ask Beetlebah to push Juliana back and forth in the stroller for a few minutes while Alexandra and I go in and perform this simple errand.

In order to gain entrance to Italian banks you have to push a green button, step into a glass tube (which always makes me think of the Orgasmatron in Woody Allen's film *Sleeper*) let the door of the tube circle closed behind you, push another button, wait for a red light to turn green, and a door to circle open in front of you, then step into the lobby. We do this. We take our ticket and get in line. All three tellers are busy with customers, so we wait. Five minutes go by. Ten minutes. I am still a little wobbly on my feet. Alexandra fidgets. The tellers are talking with each other. The customer at the middle window is making faces and hanging his head. The tellers talk on. We wait. At last, our number appears on a screen above the tellers' heads, and Alexandra and I approach the designated window. I take out the Travelers Cheque and my passport and set them on the marble counter in front of me. The teller is smoking. He picks up the cheque ("Same as cash the world over.") and examines it. He looks across at his comrade. "Do we accept these?"

His comrade gives a discreet shake of the head.

The man looks at me kindly and says, "You have to go to our other branch. They handle the foreign exchange. The branch is just on the other side of the square. Right there. Just over there. They'll change this for you."

We go out and explain the situation to my mother.

"When are we going to McDonald's?" Alexandra wants to know, a fair question. It's possible that I should have stayed in bed because I suddenly feel like vomiting into the gutter. Juliana wants to get out of the stroller, which is not a problem; then she wants me to carry her, which is. "Up on Dada."

Dada picks her up and staggers forward.

Just a little ways along the block is another bank, not connected to the first. McDonald's is just behind us, and Alexandra has turned around and is looking back there at a toy bear on a light pole blowing actual bubbles, and two acrobatic boys doing some kind of break dance on the sidewalk in the square. These boys fall onto their backs and spin to a radio that's playing American music with obscene lyrics. We go in through another safety door and wait in another line. While we are waiting I see a bank employee walk past and I say, *"Scusi. Accetate i Travelers Cheques?"*

And he says, *"Sì, sì,"* and points to the window.

"They accept them here," I tell Alexandra. "We're all set. We'll get some money and go right to McDonald's, and after McDonald's, we'll go to the ice cream place you like."

She says, "I have to go potty, Dad."

"Okay, can you hold it for just a few minutes?"

"I think so."

We go up to the teller, who is smoking, and I put the Travelers Cheque and my passport on the marble counter between us. He takes a pull on the cigarette (Alexandra is holding her

142

breath, then pretending to cough, loudly, then casting dirty looks up in this man's direction), blows smoke over his shoulder, and picks up the Travelers Cheque. After examining it he says to the teller at the next window; "Paolo, do we take these?"

"Only if they have an account here," Paolo says, without looking at me.

Our teller gives the cheque another going-over, takes another puff from his cigarette. Alexandra is tugging on my shirtsleeve. "Dad, why is he smoking?"

"I don't know, Honey."

"Dad, I'm hungry. My tummy hurts. And I have to go potty."

"One second, one second."

"Do you have an account here?" the teller asks.

"Of course I don't have an account here. I live ten thousand miles away. Listen, these cheques are as good as cash all over the world. I have my passport. Here."

"Have you tried the bank over there?" he says, pointing back to the place we just left.

"Yes. They told me to go to their other branch."

He lifts his eyebrows as much as to say, "Why didn't you then?"

"Daddy!"

"One minute, Honey."

"I'm sorry. We can't cash this."

"Fine. I want to talk to a supervisor."

The man seems untroubled by this. He motions for Alexandra and me to walk around and meet him in back, which we do. By this time, I am muttering rather loudly, in English. I meet the gray-shirted teller at a door to an office. He gives two perfunctory knocks and walks in, and I walk in right behind him. At the desk sits an official of the bank, a man, in a brown suit, straight out of the pages of Nikolai Gogol. He does not look at me. Our teller explains the situation to him, and, as if he has been trained for such eventualities, as if he has been through this a thousand times and is now merely exercising the authority that has been vested in him, as if he has earned an advanced degree in this very aspect of the banking business, he says, "Go ask the Director."

The gray-shirted teller makes a "follow me" motion with his arm. He is kind. He is all kindness. He leads us across the lobby, down a short corridor, and to another door. Someone is standing outside the door. The Director, this someone tells us, is upstairs, at a meeting.

The teller turns to us, all apologies, kind as can be. "I can't make this decision, the Director has to make it."

"Where is the Director?"

"Upstairs. In a meeting."

"When will he be back?"

"I can't say. Soon."

"How soon? Five minutes? Twenty minutes?"

"I can't say. But wait here, he'll be here soon."

"Dad, I'm hungry. Dad?"

"But this is as good as cash," I say, too loudly, waving the cheque between us. "Everywhere in the world that I have ever been!"

"I'm sorry."

The teller goes back to his window, leaving us there in the corridor, facing the blank wooden door. There is a bathroom, at least, and we use it.

"Stupid, stupid system, stupid," I'm saying, loudly, as Alexandra and I abandon all hope and go back out through the safety door.

My mother is waiting patiently on the sidewalk.

"*Now* can we have lunch, Dad?"

"Hahbug, hahbug. Fench fies!"

We try the second branch of the first bank. We go in. We wait in line. We are rebuffed without even a reference to the Director and so we decide to take refuge in the Bancomat. We don't care what the rate of exchange is, what kind of usurious commission the machine will take. We want cash, now. Cash, food, someplace to sit and practice sphincter contractions.

On the sunny sidewalk in front of the Bancomat stands a man holding his credit card in one hand. On this man's face is a look of utter helplessness, of defeat. He tries his card again; the machine rebuffs him, dismisses him, fends off his well-meaning advances. He looks at me plaintively.

"Non funzione?" I say.

He shrugs. It seems he is about to cry. He gestures for me to give my card a go. I do, and the machine churns for a few seconds, grinds, buzzes, spits out 250 Euros, and I turn away before I can see the first tears.

But the young woman behind the counter in McDonald's is friendly, and lets us leave the stroller there, in the busy lobby, while we take our Happy Meals downstairs to the dining area. I barely have enough strength to open the little ketchup packets and squirt them on the kids' cardboard-box plates. They are ecstatic and eat with a healthy appetite. They are ecstatic when we stop for ice cream cones, too. There is no place to sit and eat them and so we carry them to a little wall overlooking the Roman amphitheater.

We walk back to the apartment, pushing the stroller through the cobbled streets, and meet Amanda there, pleased from her day, refreshed, smiling her lovely smile. I go back to bed.

21

I get up in the early evening and shuffle back and forth across the apartment's tiled floor, drinking bottled water. Amanda prepares a dinner of pork chops and broccoli, pasta on the side, and I sit at the table in the magnificent dining room and watch my family eat. The flu seems to have returned. Then again, I tell myself, watching Juliana clean her pasta plate, a flu can sometimes seem to grow stronger just before it subsides. King of optimism.

We get the girls to bed, put down folded blankets beside Alexandra's in case she falls out again, and sing to Juliana in her crib. My mother reads for half an hour, then wishes me a quick recovery and kisses us good-night. Just before bedtime Amanda says, "Someone is having a bonfire or something in the back courtyard."

I open the little window near the bathroom—a place where I've been spending a lot of time—and look straight down. There, in our small back courtyard/alleyway, a knot of men I assume to be Bangladeshi crouch around a flame, the smell of cooking lamb and beans rising up against the side of the building. On our previous Italian vacation, in Rome, I stopped to talk to a young Bangladeshi man who was selling trinkets— mechanical soldiers—just in front of the Roman Forum, and he told me what it had been like to leave his country and make the treacherous overland journey across Asia, Russia, and Europe and down the Italian peninsula. "Italy is the only place the police didn't beat us," he said, and looking down at the knot of émigrés I think: God bless them. Let them eat. Let them not burn the building down, and not get in trouble for the fire, and not be sick and not be hungry and not be persecuted. Let them eat.

Having offered up this little prayer, I brush my teeth, then begin to shake so violently that I can't pour water into a cup without spilling it. It's as if someone has connected me to an electric outlet—no pain, just a hard shaking that knocks my teeth together. Amanda is in the other room, but she's endured enough bad health reports over the past two weeks, so I quietly take two ibuprofen and stand in the bathroom doorway, trying to will my body to be still. When I move in the direction of the bedroom, Amanda notices. I tell her I'll be all right, and climb into bed, where I shake and twitch for another twenty minutes, before falling into the deepest sleep I've had since crossing the Atlantic.

The next day I am hungry, a good sign. I manage to eat a brioche and some fruit for breakfast. During the meal—loud and happy and full of activity as always, thanks to our energetic offspring (did Amanda and I move around this much when we were one and five?)—my mother and I decide we will play in the golf tournament that is being held out at the local *piccolo* course.

"Are you sure, Rol?" she says, after we've talked about it for a while.

"I'm fine. Something washed out of me last night. I feel different."

"Why don't you just go and play by yourself. It's going to be all men. I won't feel right."

But Amanda and the girls have plans to go off to a seaside city called Otranto, which the guidebook calls "worth a visit."

The main attractions of Otranto seem to be a twelfth-century mosaic, and a wall lined with the 800 skulls of city residents massacred when the Turks invaded in 1480. I can tell that my mother would rather play golf. I can tell, partly because I'm her son, and partly because we are both addicted. This is the way the mind of the golf addict works: You haven't eaten for the previous four days; you've been spending half of that time in the bathroom and the other half in bed. You were shaking like a cell tower in an earthquake just the night before, spilling water, unstable on your feet, but someone mentioned something about a golf tournament and so, when you wake up the next morning feeling stronger, the greens and fairways whisper to you.

It's a benign addiction. To those who don't play, the sight of overweight men bouncing around in electric carts and hacking up clods of turf seems pitiable, laughable. I understand that. I have enough friends who despise the sport on principle, and who mock my passion without mercy. But, deep inside, I know that these people are missing out on one of life's treasures—an excuse to be outdoors in all weather, walking a manicured field, struggling to master an impossible physical activity, figuring distance, wind direction, club loft, the grain and slope of a green, the texture of sand in a bunker, the puzzle of the architect's intention, making a fool of yourself, laughing at yourself, encouraging your playing partners, trying and failing and trying again. And then hitting, once or twice a round, a shot that Tiger Woods or Annika Sorenstam would be pleased to hit. Really, there is nothing like it.

So Amanda and the kids drive us out to the Acaya Golf Club, which, we have been told by the people on the phone there, is a ten-minute trip. By helicopter, perhaps. By Kangoo, it takes just under half an hour. But we find Acaya without a bit of trouble, and turn down the long access road that runs through a stretch of sandy land textured with cactus and other desert flora. From the parking lot, Acaya seems like a real course—golf carts lined up outside, fairways, greens, and bunkers spread out over a dry, gently-rolling landscape, flags snapping in the wind. We go into the clubhouse and sign up for the tournament. The wind is blowing at a steady twenty miles an hour, but the day is sunny. We are matched up with a club member, a good golfer, a man with a substantial belly, a handsome face, and an intent manner that precludes much conversation. Fine by us. Still shaky from the week of undernourishment, I stand up on the first tee and pull my drive well left, into a lake. I am happy.

The Acaya Golf Club course is not *piccolo*, not in the slightest. It is, in fact, a difficult, beautifully-laid-out, full-length, eighteen-hole championship course. With the wind, the unfamiliar holes, and a slightly hilly terrain marked by barrancas, brush, and water hazards, it's all the challenge my mother and I could ask for. And it is a deep pleasure, after the trials of the past week, to be swinging a club again, lining up a putt, looking out over a long, undulating swath of fairway with a four-and-a-quarter-inch target there, four hundred yards in the distance.

We play reasonably well but do not win the tournament. Our dark-haired companion does not win it either, but we shake hands all around on the last green and part company amicably enough. Afterwards, in the great Italian tradition, there's a very good spaghetti and wine lunch, with warm appetizers—eggplant, olives, mushrooms—spread out on a buffet table. Looking at this feast, one has the sense that the golf was secondary, a sort of opening act, an obligatory prelude to the main event: eating. My mother and I join in the meal, indulge in an afternoon glass of wine, talk over some of our shots and finish things off with a cappuccino. No nausea afterwards, a good sign.

When Amanda picks us up in the parking lot, everyone seems fairly happy. "How was Otranto?" I ask her. She just shakes her head.

"The beach was filthy, Daddy," Alexandra says. "There were bottles and papers everywhere. Why do people do that?"

22

One of the nicest things about Lecce—and, as my strength returns, Juliana regains her full form, and the temperature climbs another few degrees, we become better acquainted with the city—is the *pasticceria* just a hundred meters down Palmieri Street from our palace. In the mornings, after the girls and I have brushed our teeth, washed our faces, and spent a quarter of an hour playing hide and seek in an apartment that seems to have been designed for it, Alexandra and I walk down the forty-six steps into the echoing stone entranceway where we leave our stroller and Alessandro leaves his beaten-up bike. "Watch your head," I always say to her, because the top of the door, for some reason, is only five feet above the ground.

"I don't need to, Dad. You need to."

"All right, thanks. Hold my hand," I say, as we step out into the cool morning, because I know the day is fast coming—a year or five years or nine years down the road—where there won't be the smallest chance of her holding my hand if I ask her to. With her, and with Juliana, I have moments when I want to stop time, when I tell myself: appreciate this, be grateful for this, remember this. I can feel in my bones the way those moments are flying past, the way this warm pressure against my palm, this trust, this happy unselfconscious innocence, this beginning of a feisty independence I hope the world does not take away from her, I can feel all that racing past, a comet you glimpse for a few seconds or a few nights in the starry, cold, New England sky, or the southern Italian morning, and then lose sight of forever.

Hand in hand we go down Palmieri Street. A few cars pass us, here in the pedestrian district, their tires bubbling along the cobblestones. Workmen are chipping away with chisels at the facade of a restaurant, breaking off the soft, worn stucco so they can apply a new smooth surface. Dogs tear at bags of refuse that someone left outside the dumpster in the middle of the night—too lazy, too angry, or too weak to lift the metal top and toss in their garbage. Parents are walking their children to school. Men and women are trundling off to work behind the wheels of undersized cars that would look like toys on the American road. Someone steps out onto a second-floor balcony and gazes out at the spring morning. Alexandra takes it all in. So do I.

The Pasticceria Pietanto is a cheerful establishment, all glass walls, marble floors and chrome coffee machines in the morning sun, and a young man and young woman in white aprons behind the sparkling stone counter. There are a few Italian newspapers lying in a rack near the cash register, and I always glance at them, and the headlines are always bad. War is coming, the world feels it.

There are shelves behind the clear plastic doors of a display case at the Pasticceria Pietanto, and on these shelves we see an array of freshly cooked pastries. Each member of the family has a favorite, so my eldest daughter and I shop accordingly. Alexandra and my mother like the *ghiambelli*, a type of greasy donut coated in rough-grain sugar. Juliana likes the plain, soft rolls with their glazed skin. Amanda prefers the crunchy, sugary butterflies. And, stomach recovered now, I am a fan of the *cornetta con crema*, a cotton-soft croissant with a dollop of thick lemony cream inside. I stop at the counter to practice my Italian, have a quick macchiato with extra hot milk (Alexandra gets a sip or two), or, sometimes, a fresh-squeezed blood orange juice. Here, as is often the case in Italy, the people who serve the food do not take your money. (The Europeans have some neat sanitary regulations like this: long before the invention of bathroom sensors, they had sinks with foot petals to turn on the water, so that you didn't pass along germs via the faucets.) They wrap everything in a bag, and you carry the bag a few steps over to the cashier and are trusted to describe the contents. Alexandra hands the cashier a five-Euro bill, and the cashier hands her back the coin change, which she then hands to me. It is a simple little ritual, but it feels like something holy. On our visit to Rome, when she was only two, we had a similar morning routine. She'd be in her pajamas, still, and I'd wrap her up in my leather jacket, step out into the sunny, smoky, Roman morning, and carry her to a Mom-and-Pop convenience store a block away. We'd pick out brioches from a just-cooked selection laid out on a sheet of brown paper, the woman would reach out and pinch Alexandra's cheeks, say *"Che bella, che bellissima!"* and we'd pay and make our way happily back to our rented home.

In a kind of echo of those good days, here in Lecce we make the five-minute stroll back to the apartment, climb the stairs and show our treasures to Mom. Amanda warms the pastries in the oven. We assemble ourselves at the table and enjoy a morning feast of cereal, fresh fruit (kiwis, oranges, a sweet species of Italian apple we haven't found anywhere else) and the thick, creamy yogurt we all love.

"This place grows on you," my mother says, of the apartment. After breakfast, over my objections, she washes the dishes in a methodical fashion that might have come from her military days. She still makes her bed first thing, with military corners, and shows the girls how to do it. She packs her suit-case neatly, gets to places on time and with a good attitude, never complains, pays for meals, helps out with the girls, suf-fers through my moods and our marital spats without com-ment, and asks only to be rewarded with the occasional church visit or nine holes of golf.

While she works, I play another round of hide-and-seek with the girls. The apartment has indentations near the win-dows, covered by floor-length drapes, and stone nooks and crannies everywhere, empty closets, a shower stall in one bath-room, beds you can easily crawl under, even a door from our bathroom that leads into a little outdoor enclosure—four walls, no ceiling—where we hang out clothes to dry. Juliana doesn't like to hide alone, and she and Alexandra don't like it if my hid-ing place is too good, and they can't find me within a minute or two. "Make some noise, Dad," they'll call, and I'll chirp or grunt or whistle from beneath one of the beds or behind a cur-tain.

Today is the day for Amanda to join in the golfing fun. She and my mother will play the first nine, and then Beetlebah and I will play the second. We finish the hide-and-seek, pack up the Kangoo with essentials and head out of town on another sunny day. I drop them at the course (Alexandra will go along for the pleasure of riding in the electric cart), against Juliana's big-lunged objections. The wind is blowing hard as ever, but the course is empty of other golfers on this morning, and Gabriele, who mans the desk, is bespectacled, proper, and welcoming. "SEE MAMA! SEE MAMA!" Juliana screams when we part company, so instead of driving away immediately, she and I sit in the Kangoo in the gravel lot until we see the three Merullo ladies putter up to the first tee. Then I drive her out the long access road, and we head south, down the Salento shoreline.

The coast here is as picturesque as the guidebooks promised it would be. The sea is a translucent aquamarine, and clean (cleanest water in Europe, some locals tell us, though the beaches, in the off season at least, are coated with litter. People we meet in Lecce say this is because the cruise ships dump their trash at sea shortly after leaving port and it washes back ashore on this coast). Though the land is rather flat, it is not so flat as to be featureless: there are small rises and dips here and there, barrancas, sloughs, sandy berms, olive groves, a wide variety of shrubs and one or two mysterious, pricey villas set behind locked iron gates. Now that the illness has passed, our decision to leave the mountains and make the long drive to this place seems like a wise one.

We turn onto a dusty road that runs toward the water across an undulating field of dead coral. We park near the sea, and Juliana and I sit back in the sun and catch up on our sleep. Near noon when I wake, she is still dozing, and I take the car gently back to the pavement and head into Melundugno for lunch.

Melundugno is one of the places we thought about living when we were still in the researching phase of things—before Contigliano, before Florida. On one of those frigid Massachusetts nights, working the Internet in my upstairs office, I found a realtor in Lecce, and made contact. When she wrote back, I told her what we were looking for, and she went up and down this stretch of coastline—on her computer and in her car—checking out possibilities. At one point she sent an email saying, "I think this would be right for you." The pictures included in that email were of a two-story beach house, newly stuccoed, with a gated parking area below, a small garden, and a clean, well-lit interior. "It's just on the outskirts of Melundugno," she wrote, but when we found out that Melundugno would be mostly empty at that time of year, we decided to pass. "That's all right," she wrote back. "I'm just happy you and your family are coming to Italy!"

As we turn into Melundugno, I am thinking of her. Juliana wakes from her hap, and I say a prayer of thanks that we didn't rent the house here. The town seems to be completely deserted, like parts of Martha's Vineyard in January. I coast down a few streets, past unoccupied houses and empty front yards. A filigree of blown sand decorates the edges of the pavement. At last, I see a man out in front of one of the houses, and stop to ask him if there might be a place to get some lunch not too far away.

"*Certo*," he says, happy to be of assistance. "Of course. Go to the end here, go left into the center, then go right, you'll see a *trattoria*."

I go here to the end. I go left into the center where there are a few stores that seem to be open. I go right along this commercial street—the ocean is just beyond this row of buildings, you can feel it—and I see a fellow in a sport coat walking along on his mid-day errands. I stop and ask him about places to eat. He starts to give directions, then changes his mind, cuts across in front of the car and waves for me to follow. We go down the half-deserted main street in this strange formation: the man striding briskly along between my left front wheel and the sidewalk, purposefully, helpfully, as if leading a horse he thinks might bolt for the fences. And the hungry American, full of hope, guiding the Kangoo along beside him at five miles an hour. A hundred feet of this and my guide sees someone lingering on the corner and shouts: "Alfredo! This fellow wants to eat in your restaurant!"

I thank him. Alfredo shows me where to park, and I worry for a moment that this is going to be another one of those cases where someone has hooked a tourist and delivered him to the door of another desperate-for-business restaurateur who happens to be married to his cousin, and who passes his day standing out on the sidewalk waving his arms at any car with people in it. Would you like to eat here or near the water? Would you like the octopus. No? Alright then we'll cook some up for you. Of course we take credit cards.

But Alfredo isn't like that. Alfredo's restaurant is empty, true; and the TV is on too loud. But the place has a vibrant look to it, with potted plants catching rays of sun, and a gleaming copper cappuccino machine behind the bar. Alfredo himself is like a gentle spring breeze, deferential, professional, calm as a beach at sunset. "FENCH FIES! FENCH FIES!" Juliana is shouting. Alfredo pinches her cheeks, brings us bread, wine, water, then French fries, a plate of thin, spicy, grilled sausages, a fresh salad. On the TV in front of us there is reportage about the impending war, and about a pileup of cars in the fog on the Autostrada outside Venice. Eighteen people have been killed.

Alfredo watches the bad news from his post near our table. We fall into conversation. It turns out he used to work in Davos, Switzerland, and has served meals to the likes of Henry Kissinger and Eduard Shevardnadze. He exhibits that agreeable combination of someone who is aware of the wider world, on the one hand, curious about it; and, on the other, fully centered and content in his own little corner of things. "In the summers," he tells me, "this town is full to overflowing. My restaurant is busy day and night."

When I ask for coffee, he says, "Certainly. And the coffee you won't pay for, not in my restaurant." There it is again, I want to say to Juliana, the Italian generosity reflex, antidote to the pettiness of the world, a gesture, a belief system: people first. I grew up with that, I want to say. It sleeps in me; on some days it wakes up and shows the world its happy face. I want to pass that on to you if I can, you and your sister. I'll try to pass that on.

We pay and go back out into the sunny little town and I

find myself replaying the Contigliano adventure and thinking: maybe Melundugno wouldn't have been so bad after all.

Back at Acaya, we make the transfer, and Beetlebah and I play the back nine in the wind and sun while Amanda and the girls check out another section of coastline. During this half-round of golf the fairway gods shower me with blessings. I play better than I have ever played in my life, smashing straight drives into the teeth of the wind, lofting crisp irons onto the green, sinking putts. Two birdies in nine holes, a personal record to that point in my golfing life. I finish two over par in the stiff breeze, Beetlebah plays solid golf, as always, and we ride back to Lecce with Amanda and the girls in a warm bath of contentment. Whatever bad cloud has been hovering over us, whatever bad spell we have been under, seems to have lifted.

23

**But, though we knock the idea back and forth for a while
that night, there is really no chance of staying in Lecce a
second week.** Even at Giorgio's bargain rate, the wonderful
apartment is a stretch for us financially. And the city, though
we've come to like it well enough, isn't someplace we feel we
can enjoy for another seven or eight days. Amanda and I talk
about it after our own fashion, pros and cons, the well-being of
the girls, my mother, our bank account, such as it is. In the
end, I go down to the little copy shop on our block, where the
owner lets us use his dial-up Internet service for six dollars an
hour, and I send a note to the travel agent at home, telling her
we need to move up our return date.

This feels like defeat. Amanda and I have traveled hundreds of thousands of miles together, living in windowless,
four-dollar-a-night Mexican motel rooms, and cramped Russian hotels where the heat and hot water were unpredictable
and the food awful. We've found our way back and forth
across Europe and America a couple of times, without reservations, plans or contacts, fitting meals and lodging into tight and
not-so-tight budgets, figuring train schedules, changing a flat
tire on a rented car in Rome, sleeping in an Olds Ninety-Eight
in rural Mississippi, swimming in icy Bavarian lakes, making
bed and breakfast arrangements on the spot in Slovenia, without sharing more than two words of any language with the

proprietor. Against the advice of good friends, we took Alexandra to Italy twice when she was very young—diapers, medicines, folding crib, stroller—and never regretted it, never thought: our friends were right, we should have taken her to Disneyworld. And we've never given up on a trip, never come home early, never been so battered—emotionally, physically, financially—by a traveling adventure that we threw in the towel and retreated to the comforts of home.

But this time we do. Even with the good day in Melundugno, and the exceptional half-round of golf, I see that something in me has been turned to ash. Temporarily, I hope, but some enthusiasm for the road, even for Italy, has perished.

As a kind of punishment for this lapse of faith, the traveling gods inform us, via the dial-up Internet connection in the little copy shop, that we will have to pay two hundred dollars per ticket to change the date of return. Only a little less than it would cost us to stay in Lecce another week. Even so, we decide to do it.

24

So, naturally, not long after we admit to ourselves that our enthusiasm for the road has dried up, we decide to take a ride. It is our next to the last day in Lecce. I agree to take this ride against my better judgment. Amanda, I know, wants badly to see the little town of Alberobello, and the *trulli* there, igloo-like buildings made from local stones, without mortar. The *trulli* were written up in the *New York Times* travel section, and we've kept the clipping, and they look, from the photos in that article, like fascinating structures. I am sympathetic. But, I tell her, we're about to set forth on a five-hundred-mile drive north, and every tourist attraction so far, from Otranto to the Florence of the South itself, has been either a mild or a major disappointment. The kids are car-weary, as is my mother. We knock it back and forth. In the end, for some reason known only to God, we go.

I don't want to talk about the trip to Alberobello. It is too painful to talk about, really, just when our bad luck, spawned by bad decisions, seemed to have swum far out to sea. Suffice it to say that the trip to Alberobello is an unmitigated disaster. Suffice it to say that, in fact, we never even make it to Alberobello.

A few days earlier, when we had just decided to abandon ship and change our return date, we'd been told by the not particularly friendly people in a Lecce travel agency (which will remain unnamed) that we would have to go to an airport in order to get the tickets changed. I think now, that if I could alter one aspect of the Italian character, it would be to encourage those fine and warm people to include, as a sort of footnote to their well intended advice, either the phrase, "I don't know", or the caveat, "But I am not sure." If the person at the travel agency in Lecce that shall go unnamed had said, for example: "We can't change the tickets for you here. *I think* you have to go to an airport and change them at the Al Italia desk, *but I am not sure.*" How nice that would have been. It would have been nice for us because, trusting souls that we are, we believed we were being given accurate information, and so we headed off to the nearest airport with an Al Italia office.

For some peculiar reason, though Lecce is a large city with a good-sized airport served by the national airline, Al Italia does not have an office there. The nearest airport with an Al Italia office turns out to be in Brindisi, one hour to the north. So, weary of the road though we all are, we head off to Brindisi on another sunny, windy day, to officially change our return date to America.

The Brindisi airport, it should go without saying, is on the north side of the city, and we are coming up from the south. We have a little adventure getting out of Lecce, because there is a construction project going on near the gate to the historical center and all the traffic lights are out of order. This makes for a kind of Intersection Roulette and I enjoy myself.

After surviving our first round of Intersection Roulette, we head north and drive for almost an hour. We loop around the outskirts of Brindisi on a sort of ring road, follow the signs for "Aeroporto" (which, to our alarm, suddenly change to "Aerostazione" at the next to the last moment) and turn down an access road, past Uzi-toting soldiers, into the parking lot. We leave the girls in the car with my mother (made somewhat

162

uneasy, understandably enough, by the Uzi-toting soldiers) and go into the modest terminal. By some lucky chance, there is no one in line at the Al Italia desk. And by some even luckier chance, the clerk on duty there is a white-headed, kind-faced fellow named Bellini (the name of my favorite Italian painter) who listens patiently to our broken Italian. Signore Bellini examines the tickets, punches something into his computer, studies the screen, makes a face, and tells us he is sorry but the tickets cannot be changed there. We will have to contact the agency in America where they were purchased. The agency will change them—there will perhaps be a fee—and everything then will be all set, *tutto a posto*.

So, having accomplished nothing, we drive all the way back to Lecce.

I mention this little side trip only because it bears on the drive to Alberobello, which I do not want to mention. The side trip to the Aerostazione bears on the trip to Alberobello like so: there are two ways to go toward Alberobello from Lecce. One way is to go north to Brindisi, along the shore, and then cut inland. This route has the advantage of offering you a trip along faster highways. The other way—which has no advantages—is to go directly north from Lecce on smaller, inland roads. On the day we make our ill-fated drive to Alberobello, I choose the second way, insist on it, in fact. I have already made the coastal drive to Brindisi, two hot hours in the Kangoo with no result; it has unpleasant associations. It was only two days ago, and I remember very well how it felt to be driving home in the sun, lugging the girls and my mother two hours for no reason whatsoever. So I vote for the inland roads, and convince Amanda it makes sense.

For the first half hour or so, this works out fairly well. We make it safely past the non-working stoplights a second time and shoot out into the countryside. The smaller roads are emp-

163

ty enough, we get lost only twice, and each time only briefly. But, after an hour in the hot car, it becomes apparent to us that Alberobello is perhaps three times farther away from Lecce than we've been told it is. Why this comes as a surprise to me, I can't imagine.

A Lecce acquaintance had said that, if we made the trip to Alberobello, we should stop in Ostuni, which she described as a pretty city of white hillside houses. We do that. We find a parking space there. We find a place to eat. We take a small walk and then get back on the road, Alberobello in our sights.

We follow signs that lead us to other signs, that lead us to . . . signless intersections. It is hot in the car. The kids are particularly fussy (These things, it seems to me, have a sort of biorhythm all their own: most of the time the girls get along fine, are easily pleased, and then there will be these flare-ups of discontent, with each other, with the trip, with the rules set down by their mild-mannered parents. The timing of all this is a mystery; it seems to be a world in microcosm. Why do wars start when they do? Why do lovers cruise along happily for a day or a week or a month and then break out into arguing?)

Amanda wants to stop and take photographs of the intricate, hilly landscape, and I oblige her at first, sitting in the car with the children complaining, and my mother suffering in silence, and the sun beating down. What must it be like to live here in the heat of summer? But a small fire of annoyance is being stoked in me. It is not easy, traveling with a photographer. Landscape that is merely pleasing to your eye is compelling to hers. She wants to stop, wander around, get the right angle, the right light, just the right shot. And you want to enjoy the landscape while you're moving. We've had this particular disagreement on other trips, even before there were complaining children in the back seat. And now the memories of those arguments circle back, like vultures sniffing blood.

164

When we actually begin to come upon some *trulli* in the ancient vineyards by the sides of the road, things get more complicated. These are interesting enough little structures, resembling nothing we've ever seen. Small miracles of masonry, you might say. You might slow down a moment, perhaps stop for one quick closer look and a snapshot. Unless you are a professional photographer. In which case you suspect you will never see any *trulli* at home, never see them anywhere else on earth, in fact. You want to find just the perfect *trullo*, and then you want to get out and walk around it, looking for just the perfect angle, waiting for a cloud to pass and the sun to come out again. And, though you have two kids, a cranky husband, and a silent mother-in-law in the hot Kangoo, you become so absorbed in framing the *trulli* just so, in just the right light, that you forget about everything else.

The roads grow more serpentine, the kids grow hotter, their complaints taking on—at two very different levels of verbal ability—that awful whiny note known to every parent. "Dad, it's hot it's hot it's hot, agggh!" "Up, up, UP! DadEEE!" And so on.

At last, an hour or so outside of Ostuni, when we have been winding along the Puglian roads and negotiating photography stops, and when I have been feeling the girls' pain, and listening to them express that pain, and been worrying about my mother's comfort, I reach the bottom of my reservoir of marital and parental good will. "We're not going to Alberobello," I declare suddenly. "We'll go to Martina Franca, then we'll go home."

Amanda greets this pronouncement with a deadly silence. I know I am wrong. She knows she is wrong. The kids know both of us are wrong. No good solution presents itself.

I make the turn to Martina Franca. "Martina Franca is supposed to be nice, too," I say, in a gesture of reconciliation.

"Alberobello is supposed to be a tourist trap."

Silence.

"Alright, how about this: you find the best goddamned *trulli* you can, and we'll stop for ten minutes and you can take all the goddamned pictures you want, and then we'll go back to Lecce, and even then we're not going to get the kids home in any reasonable time for dinner and bed."

Silence.

By the time we stop in Martina Franca, which is, in fact, a perfectly interesting town with white stucco buildings standing along curving streets and a sense of leisureliness about it that some spa towns have, by the time we stop there for the promised ice cream, my reservoir is not only dried up, the walls have begun to crack. Things are so bad that, while the rest of the crew goes into a nearby cafe for *gelato* and coffee, I ignore the calls of my legendary sweet-tooth, step into a small church and sit in one of the pews there. At that moment I am so far from God I can't pray, cannot even plead for a quick, safe trip back to Lecce. I simply sit and stare at the mural above the altar.

In a while, I hear my beautiful children skipping through the door, saving me from myself yet again; the reservoir begins to refill. Alexandra comes up to me and says: "Dad, someone in the cafe made Juliana cry. He was trying to joke with her but he did it in a scary way."

"Glad I wasn't there," I say. "You want to light a candle?"

On the long ride back to Lecce, Amanda is silent at first, then says, "I was selfish." I say nothing. We find our way back to Via Palmieri and leave the car there. Ma is too tired for dinner, and goes upstairs to rest. Amanda and the girls and I go in search of a place to eat, but none of the restaurants will open until it is past their bedtime, so we settle for some mini-sandwiches at the Pasticceria Pietanto, a slice of pizza for Alexandra, and a two-dollar bottle of Primitivo for me.

It has not been the best of days. We will survive. The kids will sleep and wake up refreshed. Beetlebah's energy will return. As we have done for twenty-some years, Amanda and I will forgive each other our selfish spots, our quirks and moods, our bad decisions made with good intentions. This is the complicated dance of family life, made to a sweeter tune on some days than on others. But it will be months before either of us says the word "Alberobello" again in the other's presence.

25

The next morning, the morning of our departure from the Florence of the South, it turns out that Amanda has somehow injured her back. She has been lifting Juliana into and out of the Kangoo for three weeks now, lugging the camera bag, grocery bags, golf bags. By the time we get home, this injury will have become so troublesome that, for the first time in her life she will require codeine and chiropractor visits.

It doesn't seem wise for her to lift anything heavy, so we pack our belongings into the suitcases and I start carrying them downstairs. Nineteen bags in all. Forty-six steps each way. I carry our bags in the order in which they must be placed in the Kangoo so they will fit. The first large duffel bag that has most of the kids' clothes in it. Forty-six steps down and forty-six empty-handed steps back up. The second duffel bag. Forty-six down and forty-six steps back up. By the time I get to the golf bag, last on the list, my legs are shaking and my lungs hurt but we're ready to go. And we're hopeful. I am hopeful, at least. I believe it is still somehow possible to build on the basically good week in Lecce and rescue the vacation, to make these final five days into something like whipped cream and a maraschino cherry . . . placed neatly on top of sour and freezer-burned scoops of pistachio ice cream.

The plan is as follows: we will break the long drive north into five segments, traveling only three or four hours each day.

We have purchased a book that lists all known Italian *agriturismos*, so there will be no more intuition-sponsored searches for imaginary ones. Each night we will stop at one of these actual *agriturismos*, salving our wounds in pretty scenery, soft beds, and exceptional meals. That is the plan, and it is a good one.

During our last hour in the palatial suite of rooms, Alexandra makes a homemade card for Alessandro in the apartment downstairs. We have seen him only in passing, but I'm hoping that this token of her affection and warmth will somehow act as a sort of talisman and keep him out of trouble in the years to come. If it prevents him from slamming a soccer ball against the neighbor's lacquered door, even for one afternoon, then we shall have left our mark on the Florence of the South. We fold the card around an American dollar, slip it under his door, drop the apartment keys with a friend of Stefano's near the Porta Napoli, and head out, through the traffic-light roulette, north and west.

According to our map, which is a good map, really, a German-made fold-up with a scale of 1:600,000 (a number that means nothing to me but that looked impressive when we bought the map) . . . according to this map, there is a fairly major highway heading north and west from Lecce, toward the city of Taranto. In this, the map proves to be accurate. For the first forty-five minutes we motor along, making good time, cutting through dusty, simple, interesting little towns and then hurrying out into the flat countryside again. Juliana is singing along to the "Bah Bah Black Sheep" tape and asking for digestive crackers. My mother and Alexandra are working on word games. Amanda is studying the map, checking it against the *agriturismo* guide, and calculating likely places to stop on our first night.

We have more or less already recovered our domestic equilibrium, performed the small miracle that billions of families perform, all over the globe, during any given week: we have argued and gotten ugly and faced despair and regret and then stepped back from all that and made a decent peace. We will be in Taranto for lunch.

Except that, near the tiny town of San Pancrazio, we encounter an unexpected detour for road construction. This puts us at the mercy of the sign-artists. We turn right at the first orange DEVIAZIONE sign, go five miles, see a second orange sign, turn left, go through the small town, see another orange sign, come to a T . . . No more signs. This happens four times, in slightly different configurations. Four. An hour later, when we at last rejoin highway 7*ter*, (I don't know what the "ter" is for, but that's the way the map distinguishes it from the larger route 7) we are something like eight miles closer to Taranto. The driving on these narrow roads is difficult, with trucks racing past in the opposite direction, and speedsters riding your bumper, and the poor signage, and the creeping hunger, and the unpredictable noise levels inside the car. We go on.

In the city of Manduria, we follow the signs for Route 7ter and are led in an enormous rectangle around the outskirts. We are truly hungry now, tired of sitting, tired of word games, very tired of the "Bah Bah Black Sheep" tape.

At last, more than an hour later than we'd originally planned, we cross two bridges over the port of Taranto, and Dad promises we will turn off at the next small city and have lunch. We take the exit for the next small city, St. Palagiano, clearly marked as being six kilometers away—and wander in the countryside there for half an hour, trying to find it, trying to find anything. U-turns, curses, close calls at stop signs. The "Bah Bah Black Sheep" tape is turned off with one poke of a finger. All word games have ceased. Amanda has given up on the 1:600,000 scale folding German map of Italia, and there is no one on these country roads of whom we might inquire.

We take a wrong turn and see a sign for Castellanetta, right on the Golfo di Taranto, and soon we are driving the tree-lined streets of what is apparently a summer resort. Lots of advertisements for hotels and beaches and . . . not one open restaurant. I pull into a gas station and ask, and the attendant points us down a road that seems to lead nowhere. But, out of options, we keep going along this road and it actually ends at a hotel, only place in town that is serving lunch.

And the lunch is superb. Even with the truck drivers smoking on the other side of the dining room, even with the TV showing war preparations and anti-US demonstrations around the world. Even with all that, here in Castellanetto we find the kind of lunch you expect to find in Italy: just-baked bread, fresh salad with good olive oil, spaghetti with clam sauce that sings out a beautiful melody in your mouth, dishes of apples and pears, good local white wine, friendly waitress, a bathroom with a changing table. To use the vernacular of the New Age: all our needs are met.

It feels good to have our needs met. We enjoy the meal, let the kids run around a bit, then get back into our trusty Kangoo, back on the road, and find the highway that runs north, into the mountains, toward Potenza.

26

In a short while we leave the province of Salento and cross over into Basilicata. In his memoir, *Christ Stopped at Eboli*, Carlo Levi described his year of exile in Basilicata, which, in addition to a previous imprisonment, was his punishment for speaking up against Mussolini's dictatorship. In those days, 1935 and 1936, this part of southern Italy was desperately poor, many of the peasants sleeping in caves at night and toiling in malaria-infested fields during the day. Their lives were controlled by corrupt tax collectors and merciless local bureaucrats (who answered, if they answered to anyone, only to a madman in Rome) and a rigid class system about one half of one notch preferable to outright slavery. Anyone who ever wonders why millions of southern Italians made the arduous journey to America in the late nineteenth and early twentieth century should read what Levi has to say about Basilicata, about Italy, in those days.

But things have changed since Mussolini was caught in a German military coat, trying to sneak into Switzerland. From the vantage point of the superhighway at least, the cities we pass in the Basilicata exhibit the sparkle of a modest prosperity. The terrain is as splendid as anything we've seen: vast slanted hills rising up from the road into dry mountainsides and then vertical cliffs. The guidebooks tell us there are prehistoric caves cut into these hills, and we see herds of sheep on the lower slopes watched over by shepherds holding crooks, as if they'd walked straight out of the Old Testament; and clusters of brown stone buildings that perch improbably, in a thousand-year-old defense posture, on crags of earth far above. Each new turn of the highway brings another striking scene.

Still, it's a long drive, and by the time we are close to our goal for that day, the city of Battipaglia, all of us are more than ready to stop. Here, not far from Naples, there are 5,000 foot mountains just to the east. A few miles to our west is the Tyrrhenian sea. With Amanda in the navigator's seat, we leave the Autostrada at the first Battipaglia exit, slip down the exit ramp, wind around a rotary, and pull into a parking lot beside two phone booths. We have had some bad luck with phone booths on this trip, but one of them has to work, I think. One of the phones does, in fact, work: the second one. I dial the number of the place we've circled in the *agriturismo* guide, and the fellow who answers tells us to wait right where we are, he will come fetch us. I am picturing a country inn set high in the hills, or perhaps an oceanfront estate remodeled to accept overnight guests. I am hoping I will hear, by the end of this day, my mother's voice saying, "I could live here, Rol. I could really live here." I am hoping for a bed and a meal that will cure Amanda's sore back.

In a few minutes, a balding, middle-aged man pulls up in a blue Lancia. I reach in through the open passenger window and shake his hand, introduce myself in a friendly way. But I'm watching him closely—we are, after all, entrusting our children's comfort to this total stranger—and he seems, at first glance, a bit too friendly, cousin to Giorgio the orthodontist and to the Monopoli conman with his octopus entree and hardworking sister.

"How far is it to your *agriturismo?*" I ask him, and something, some little rodent of discomfort or deceit, scampers

173

across the muscles of his face.

"Close, very close," he says. "Just follow me."

His name is Raffaele, and he rockets out of the parking lot as if he's trying to lose us.

"My God, look at him go," my mother says.

I'm moving the shift and working the Kangoo's clutch like someone taking his final examination at NASCAR training school, flying around corners on the outside edges of the tires, running my fender within inches of oncoming trucks. It's fun. It wakes me up. "He says it's only five minutes from here," I tell Amanda giddily on a straight, fast stretch of road with no line marking the center of it. Which means that vehicles play a Battipaglian version of chicken, taking up a little more territory than they're entitled to, pushing oncoming traffic a few centimeters toward the weedy shoulder at sixty miles an hour. When this kind of thing seems like wholesome family entertainment, you know you've been in Italy too long.

"I guess we must get out into the countryside pretty fast," I say, because if the *agriturismo* is really out in the country, and only five minutes from the phone booth, then, even at these speeds, it can't be very far from the center of the city.

But, as things turn out, Raffaele's *agriturismo* isn't really in the countryside. And, as things turn out, it isn't an *agriturismo* at all, but a plain, orange-stuccoed, three-story box beside a parking lot in a semi-industrial zone, with a sign out front that clearly reads: HOTEL.

I mutter. I curse. I consider not turning into the parking lot behind the blue Lancia, but just driving on and taking our chances.

Surfaces can deceive, though. Raffaele's twelve-room Hotel Tavernola, while perhaps not technically an *agriturismo*, will turn out to be as welcoming as any place we've stayed, and as clean as if the tile had been set the day before and washed and polished that same morning. It has what all good *agriturismos* have—a sense that there is a person, not just a corporation, looking out for your comfort.

While the gang waits hopefully in the car, Raffaele gives me a tour of two rooms on the second floor, a sort of suite set off from the hallway with its own private entrance. A bath with a tiled shower, comfortable beds, even a balcony that looks out over a long stretch of vineyards to the Bay of Naples there in the western distance. Not perfect, maybe, but perfectly adequate. Raffaele's salesman's personality has evaporated, leaving a vulnerable host. He wants me to like it, to approve, and I do. Because I tell him that our children eat early, by Italian standards, he takes me downstairs and asks the chef if it would be possible to prepare the food on a different schedule that night, even if it's just a pizza, because there are children involved here. The chef looks at me without smiling, looks back at his boss. Nods.

Tutto a posto.

We do the minimum of unpacking and rest a while, wash up, get Alexandra's chest physical therapy over with, take a short stroll. At seven-thirty we go downstairs to an elegant, partly subterranean room, with stone arches and, on the stone and stucco walls, photos of Raffaele's father, also an innkeeper. Raffaele himself hovers near the table in his sport coat and polished shoes, making sure the highchair is set up correctly, that we get accurate explanations for each item on the menu, that we are comfortable in every way. His manner is gracious, unobtrusive, just right. He knows that the chance of ever seeing us again is minuscule; we're not return business, as they say in the business. We can't tip him, he's the owner. I haven't told him that I write the occasional travel article, or even that I write at all. We're sending a little bit of money his way, but as diners trickle in, even at this early hour, it becomes obvious

175

that he's not exactly struggling here. He's just kind, decent, living out some code of hospitality, its roots in ancient soil, that his father handed down.

My mother and I order the bean and vegetable soup, thick as oatmeal, and mumble compliments between sips. The girls like the pizza. Amanda smiles over her chicken marsala. Raffaele picks out a bottle of wine he thinks I will approve of, and I do approve of it, and it's not even close to the most expensive bottle on the list, and I drink most of it myself because my mother has given up wine and coffee for Lent and because Amanda rarely imbibes.

By eight-thirty the room has filled with other diners. A man and a woman set up an electric keyboard and start to sing Neapolitan tunes (she has a voice that makes me wonder what she's doing at the Hotel Tavernola in Battipaglia) dedicating the first song "to our foreign visitors," which, we realize after a moment, means us. Happy with the music, the wine, the soup, a salad and a thick steak, and with seeing my family well fed and at peace, and with maybe, maybe, having made something fine from the remnants of a disaster, I drift back into memories of my father's family (his parents were born only about twenty-five miles from this spot) and my childhood. The people in this room seem genuinely happy, the children fussed over, the food prepared with care, the host greeting everyone, spilling his kindness over every table—and all of it causes a series of sweet echoes to sound in my inner ear. Italians haven't cornered the market on happiness, hospitality, or anything else I can think of. But they know a great deal about this particular kind of happiness and generosity, this particularly Mediterranean way of enjoying life, of pretending to oneself—to one's children, especially—that there are no hard edges lurking there beneath the good times; that people are gracious and well fed everywhere, that they will love and approve of you and go out of their way to please you and help your children.

It seems to me, during that hour and a half in the Tavernola's restaurant, that I grew up surrounded by this exact kind of lie: the adults in my family, even the older cousins, offered an impossible love and generosity, as if showing me: this is the way the world can be, people can love you like this. It isn't true, of course: the world isn't that way. Only a handful of people will ever be able to offer you anything like that kind of love, and, even then, only intermittently, imperfectly. But there was a heroic effort involved, a desperate wish that the world would be different than it actually is. My grandparents, aunts, and uncles considered it their duty to bathe me and my twenty-eight first cousins in a belief in joy and goodness, and I feel it now, in this five-hundred-year-old underground room, as clearly as if it is a child's skin against my own.

I go upstairs and help Amanda put the girls to bed, kiss my mother good-night, then come down again, alone, looking for more of it. I make a present of one of my books to Raffaele, signed to him and his wife—who has just appeared and is serving as co-host. He hugs me, gives me a bottle of his own wine to take back to America. "It was alright?" He asks. *"Va bene'?"*

"Benissimo."

I tell him I want to sit down and have one small glass of anisette, but I don't tell him that anisette is what my father and his father and mother liked to drink, that the taste of it is linked, in my memory, with the impossible, mottled, imperfect promise of their affection. I sit at our cleaned and reset table, order the anisette, and insist on paying for it. I am, after all, taking up a whole table by myself, during a busy hour. But Raffaele's wife says, "We don't allow our guests to pay for these kinds of drinks."

It's impossible, of course. There is something inherently false and sentimental about such quick friendships, such reflexive concern for another's welfare—it's untested by time and moods; you don't really know the person; you could never sustain such warmth amidst the trials of everyday life. But that isn't the point. The point is the attempt—in the face of everything you know. You make a momentary connection, say nice things, offer some small gift, knowing you will never see the person again, and will forget about him or her in time. Still, you have the memory of that light shining. You have the hope of something greater, in yourself to begin with, and then, secondarily, in the world of people. You have made your small contribution to that. I finish my anisette and as I'm going out the door, Raffaele hugs me good-bye as if we are brothers.

In the middle of the night Juliana wakes up screaming. I get out of bed and walk over to her crib and put my hand on her chest, and think about the affection I received as a child, and wonder if I can pass a little of that on to her and to her sister, despite my occasional fits of impatience, my tempers and quirks and self-centeredness, and wonder if that's why I come to Italy in the first place. Not because it's cold at home, but because it's warm here.

27

In the morning, Raffaele and his wife sleep in. His mother serves us a breakfast of coffee, juice, and unlimited slices of homemade apple tort, and we say a fond good-bye to the Agriturismo Tavernola and drive on, north, toward the Eternal City.

The day is cool and very windy. On the Autostrada we pass close to Mount Vesuvius and Pompeii, and pass the long dry range of mountains that flank Rome and Naples to the east. It's impossible to number the conflicts that have taken place here, where the climate is so benign and the earth so fertile. From pre-Roman times to World War II, this soil has seen one invading army after the next, with regular volcanic eruptions in between, but we are at peace this morning.

We make it as far as Rome's ring road but then, trying to find one of the golf courses I'm supposed to play for my magazine article, we yet again become tremendously lost, spectacularly lost, going this way and that, missing signs, sailing down highway exits into clots of traffic, paying tolls we shouldn't pay, then asking the toll collector for directions to Parco de' Medici Golf Club and having him tell us to make a U-turn and come back through the toll the other way and pay again! Eventually we stop in an AutoGrill, close to missing our tee time now, maybe missing out on the small fee I stand to earn for the article. I ask directions of someone sitting in a car in the parking lot there, and the blessed man actually says, "I don't know."

At last we find the course—it is on the airport road in a patch of low-lying greenery—and my mother and I play a windy eighteen holes while Amanda drives the girls out to the ruins of the Roman settlement of Ostia Antica.

Beetlebah, at 80, is still supple and coordinated. In her youth, she was the starting third-basewoman on a team composed of some of the *League of Their Own* stars. She batted .340. Now, still, she has a beautiful golf swing, a natural coordination, and, unlike most golfers I know, an even temperament on the course. Parco de' Medici is a picturesque layout, with water on eleven of the eighteen holes, a wide variety of trees and flowering shrubs, inventively designed doglegs and par threes. On the twelfth, I make a forty-five-foot putt, something that happens maybe four times in a season. My mother follows this little bit of magic with some of her own: a thirty-five-foot putt into the same cup. We are alone in the middle of the back nine when this happens, the day is fading. The wind has died down and the slanting sunlight is dusting the willows and Italian elms with gold. I can see how happy she is, and I want to say: I am trying to pay you back here, for the two thousand miles of riding in the back seat, for all my cursing and muttering, all the disasters. There were some good times, too, weren't there? We survived, didn't we? We touch knuckles and move on to the next challenge.

We have to hurry through the last part of the back nine because a cool spring darkness is drawing down around us, so from Golf Course Parco de' Medici I will always carry an image of my eighty-year-old mother trotting across the fringe of the seventeenth green, happy as a girl in her prime, rushing to beat the end of the day.

28

I suppose I do not need to say here that we get lost on the way from the golf course to the next *agriturismo* on our list. I don't know how this happens, or why it has happened, again and again on this trip. Really, Amanda and I have decent educations and we are fairly bright people. We have a map now. We've driven hundreds of thousands of miles in rented cars all over the world without getting lost more than very occasionally. Maps, signs, guidebooks, communicating in a foreign land—we're veterans of these things, and yet, for some reason, on this trip, we can't seem to find our way from the pizza counter to the bathroom.

It's dark when we leave Parco de' Medici. Headed north through and then beyond the outskirts of Rome, carefully following, not only the directions in the *agriturismo* guide, but the clearly marked route on our excellent 1:600,000 map . . . we get lost. But we have grown humble over these past weeks: as soon as we realize we're lost we stop in a bar/restaurant and I go in and ask the bartender if I can use his phone. He says something I don't understand. I ask again. He points, shares a smirk with the three losers standing there sipping beers. I turn around and see that there is a pay phone on the wall, three feet behind me. One of the losers laughs, quietly. I call the *agriturismo* we're looking for, a place called *La Melazza*, and the man who answers speaks in a quick, slurred Italian that—over a telephone line, in a bar, with the TV on loudly—is next to impossible to decipher. *"Non capito!"* I shout into the phone. *"Non parlo molto bene' l'Italiano!"* The man behind the bar and his three friends are looking at me now as if I am a lunatic who has wandered in from the cold fields.

After a few more slurred and shouted exchanges, I get the basic drift of what's being said to me through the line. All we have to do is head north on Via Cassia, an ancient road that leads from the *gran raccordo annulare* toward the city of Viterbo. We'll see an exit for the town of Cesano. After that, just follow the signs for *La Melazza*. We can't miss it.

Fine, I say. *Va bene'*. I am about to hang up when I decide that it's probably a good idea to have him repeat these directions one more time. He does. And this time I hear: "You'll see an exit for Cesano, but don't take it. Take the next one."

"Fine. Don't take the first one," I say.

"Si, si."

Alright, nice going, I tell myself. Good thing you checked. I hang up, and, as I leave, I don't look at the man behind the bar and his three pals because I don't think it would be prudent, just then, for me to look at them. It might lead to my saying something. It might lead to my letting out some of my frustration. It might lead to several years in an Italian prison. Unfortunately, however—this happens to me on occasion, especially in buildings with which I am not familiar—I seem to have forgotten how I came into the bar/restaurant. I go out the doorway that separates the bar from the main dining area, walk across a room of empty tables, out another door, and find myself, not in the parking lot next to the Kangoo as I'd hoped, but in pitch blackness on a sort of patio surrounded by impenetrable shrubbery. At least the door hasn't locked behind me. I am able, at least, to go back into the restaurant. Totally disoriented now, I try walking in a different direction through the empty dining room, toward a different door, but this door leads into the kitchen, where I am not welcome. I go back to the bar. The man behind the bar and his three friends are watching me as if I am the best entertainment to come out of America since Jerry Lewis. I ignore them, try the third of three doors, and stumble out into the parking lot where the Kangoo sits with its flashers on. I spit on the tar there. In the darkness I make a gesture back toward my smirking friends, a rude, indecent and satisfying gesture.

"All set," I say hopefully, when I climb in behind the wheel. "We'll see an exit for Cesano, and we just take the one after that."

"Great!" Alexandra says.

"Good job, Rol," my mother says.

Juliana chimes in: "Yah Yah!"

"What will that exit say?" Amanda asks.

"I don't know. We didn't get to that. Cesano II, maybe."

Things go fairly well to start off with, in this black, moonless night. We see the first exit for Cesano.

"You're sure it isn't this one," Amanda says, and the smallest seed of doubt is planted.

I'm not in the mood for seeds of doubt, so I don't answer.

The next exit doesn't say Cesano II; it makes no reference to Cesano at all, in fact. Neither does the one after that, but we take it anyway, because now it seems (the friendly bartender had said Cesano was right around the corner) that we have certainly gone too far. We go down the dark empty ramp and there is nothing there, no signs for an *agriturismo*, no signs at all. Nothing. We drive a mile or two down the dark two-lane road that leads to the right, but see nothing that indicates an *agriturismo*. We turn around and drive up the dark two-lane road that leads to our left. We get back on the highway.

Strangely enough, the next exit we come to, heading north, says CESANO. I take it. If there's no sign at this exit, I think,

I'm just going to drive on, madly, furiously, ignoring the tiredness and hunger around me. But at the bottom of the ramp—
voila'—there's an unlit sign for *La Melazza* that Amanda somehow manages to see. We turn left, as the arrow indicates. We
loop up along a dark, hilly, country road, the wind blowing
hard now against one side of the Kangoo, no houses here, no
signs, no side streets. No bars, even, where one might inquire.

"You can't miss it," I'm muttering. "It's right around the
corner."

"What, Dad? What's right around the corner?"

"Nothing, honey."

"Daddy, what?"

"Nothing. We'll find it. We're almost there."

"Dad, what's right around the corner?"

"The *agriturismo*," Amanda says, into the dark back seat.
"Dad's just a little upset, that's all. We'll find it."

"Why are you upset, Dad?"

We go downhill, past an unreadable sign. It is a dark and
desolate road.

"That might have been it," Amanda says.

"How could that have been it? There wasn't even a road
there. If there was a road there, it would lead to nothing."

"It could have been a sign," Amanda says. "We went by it
too fast for me to be sure."

"Oh," my mother says, worried that a truck will come roaring over the hill and obliterate us as I make a U-turn and then
another U-turn across the dark road and pull up beside the
sign, if it is, in fact, a sign. It is. God is. The sign says, *La
Melazza—Agriturismo.*

"Yay!" Alexandra sings.

"Yah Yah!"

We turn down the road. It is an unbelievable road, a road
straight out of the kind of movie you see late at night on cable

TV, with vampires and ghouls and sharp knives and lots of blood: narrow, dusty, rocky, a hillside to the right and a drop-off to the left. Tremendously, unbelievably dark. There are no lights anywhere . . . except, after a minute, in my side mirror. A car is following us. This is a dead-end dirt road that leads to nothing and a car is following us. I swallow and pull over onto the shoulder. Fine, I think. This particular criminal has chosen the wrong man, at the wrong moment. If he stops and gets out I am going to rush him. I am going to rip the nearest fencepost out of the ground and hammer him. I am going to knock him like a baseball into the next *provincia*. I am going to pick him up as if he is a straw doll and fling him . . . The car passes slowly by. Headed toward *La Melazza*, no doubt.

We're moving again. Ma says, innocently, "This couldn't be the road, could it, Rol?"

But at the bottom of the dark hill, just as we have given up hope, there is another unlit sign, gates, a long dirt driveway that leads to an unmarked collection of buildings. We go up the driveway into a dirt parking area. I park, get out, and walk toward a dim lamp shining through a window in one of the buildings. The first door is locked. The second door opens when I try it and I walk into what resembles a huge wedding hall/dining room with an open stone dance floor, a coffee bar at one end, a kitchen at the other, a beautiful stone fireplace, and thirty tables covered with white cloths and silverware. Three or four people are hard at work preparing food near the kitchen. I walk up to a stocky fellow who seems to be in charge and who is missing the tip of one finger, and I introduce myself as the person who called, looking for two rooms and dinner. He does not smile. His name is Giachini. He says, "Find us alright?"

I say: "No problem."

185

29

The rooms are in a cold outbuilding, but the *La Melazza* employee who shows them to us turns on a switch outside the exterior door and promises, on the souls of all his deceased relatives, that, by the time we return from dinner, the outbuilding will be warm and comfortable. *Tutto a posto.* We go back to the large dining room and there our thick-shouldered host has undergone a transformation. Maybe it is the sight of our children, or the other children in the room. Or maybe he switches into this hospitable mode once the food is ready and the hardest work done. But now he is positively garrulous, smiling down at the girls, asking if we would like to sit next to the fireplace or over against a wall, introducing to us to an employee called Sonia, a pretty woman, thirtyish, who speaks good English.

Sonia shows us to a table and soon begins to bring us carafes—water and wine—then plates of food. First there is rolled *prosciutto*, sliced thin as a sheet of paper, enough for a football team. Then a course of grilled eggplant and omelets with spinach and olives. Then more eggplant, this course breaded and fried. At this point, with all the bread and wine, we are very close to full. But now Sonia serves us a huge plate of homemade *gnocchi* with sausage. Alexandra and Juliana have eaten all we can reasonably hope they will eat, and they've grown tired of sitting still, and are running around the dance floor with a shy Italian girl from the next table. The main course—a cut of beef—is served. We eat and eat and drink a bit, feeling the warmth of the fireplace, watching the girls play. The frenzy of the road subsides. The cold darkness seems to float away from us, away from the exterior walls of the building. Food heals. Sonia tells us there's more to come, artichokes to begin with, and then fruit, cheese, dessert. But we have to get the children to bed, and couldn't eat another bite in any case.

We roll our bodies out of the dining room and across the dark courtyard. The outbuilding is more or less warm, as promised. Diaper change, clothing change, a session of hand-washing and teeth-brushing, a quick prayer, and we are all asleep.

Next morning the sun is out and I'm still thinking about the previous night's meal. I think: we will never eat this well in America. It's somehow just not possible to eat this well, to have a meal like that and wake up feeling fine the next morning.

Through the window of our bedroom I see that *La Melazza* is set in a pretty bowl of hills, and, concerned already about my passion for food and the consequences of that, I go out for a brisk, calorie-burning walk while the rest of the clan is washing and dressing. Even now, early on a Sunday morning, a neighboring farmer is tilling his fields. I wave to the farmer, who ignores me. I think about golf, my other passion. You don't get fat from playing golf, at least.

Back in the dining room, which is completely empty now, a kindly, rotund woman makes us cappuccino and cafe latte to order, milk for the girls, and feeds us slice after slice of the apple tort she herself has made. Two apple-tort breakfasts in a row now; we could get used to this. Giachini appears, gives us a pack of Tunisian dates—no charge—and then, when he totes

187

up the bill, asks us for just about half of what the total says. I don't know why he does this—because he has taken a liking to the girls. Because having Americans at this time of year is a novelty. Because he wants to congratulate us for finding the place, reading signs in the dark, understanding his telephone Italian, and so on. Because he saw the pain and weariness on our faces when we stumbled in the night before. The entire feast for five of us, plus a night in two rooms comes to roughly $110.

"You speak Italian very well," he tells me, his speech almost as difficult to understand in person as it was on the phone.

"No, I don't. Really I don't. I wish more than anything that I did." I say I think it's a complicated and beautiful language. The verb tenses, I tell him, are especially hard to figure. (Here, for the record, are the Italian verb tenses: Present Indicative. Imperfect. Past Absolute. Future. Present Conditional. Present Subjunctive. Imperfect Subjunctive. Past Perfect. Present Perfect. Past Anterior. Future Perfect. Past Conditional. Past Subjunctive. Past Perfect Subjunctive.) He puts a hand on my shoulder and says, "Listen, even we don't know the verb tenses. They don't even teach half of those tenses in school anymore, to the kids. It's too complicated. No one uses them. In the schools now, everything is simplicity, simplicity."

I don't know if he's just trying to be kind, or if this is the truth: the beautiful language is being diluted, simplified. The food will be next.

Two of Giachini's helpers are Ukrainians, recent immigrants, and Amanda and I chat with them in Russian, another complicated, wonderful language, but one we feel more comfortable speaking. Listening to the pure accents of these women, looking at their wide faces and colorful kerchiefs, we are carried back to the years we spent in that closed-up land, where we worked on U.S. Government cultural exchange exhibits. We recall the hospitality we encountered, the almost complete absence of good food. There, in places like Rostov-on-Don, in winter especially, we learned what it feels like to eat simply to stay alive, to take no pleasure in a meal. It was, in many ways, the polar opposite to the Italian experience, though the hospitality was equally warm, and we didn't get lost as much.

We thank Giachini for the dates and the discount, compliment him for the fifth or sixth time on our dinner, bid the Ukrainians a fond *doh-svidanya*, and head off to one of Italy's ten best golf courses.

30

In case one might not already be aware of the fact that Olgiata Golf Club is one of Italy's Ten Best Courses, there are framed lists from a variety of golf magazines hanging on the walls in the club's grand lobby, providing this information in large letters. In case a visitor wonders about the status of the place, there is a gatehouse at the entrance to the community, with a guard standing there. The guard asks you your purpose and then presses a button that raises a wooden arm so you can drive up the hill, past the big homes, and into a parking lot crowded with Jaguars and Ferraris. Inside, men in two-thousand-dollar suits and women in pearls sit at felt-topped tables in the quiet card room, whiling away their Sunday morning playing tournament bridge.

But, high-status or not, Top Ten or not, on this sunny spring morning Olgiata's credit card machine is not functioning. This is too bad because, more than anything else at this point in the Italian vacation, I want one straightforward, unproblematic round of golf at a course I like. But the credit card machine is not functioning. The friendly clerks at the front desk don't admit this, of course, but make me understand that there is something faulty about my credit card. I have used this same card all over Italy, and in the U.S. as well, for months, without the smallest problem. But this fact makes no impression on the clerks at Olgiata. I take out another credit card (I

190

have a small collection), the clerk tries it, frowns down at the machine, which is printing out a message saying the card is not working. He shrugs, looks at me as if he is embarrassed . . . for me. Obviously, it is a question of my good financial standing. I ask him if he will take a check and he shakes his head, no. *Sfortunatamente.* "What about Travelers Cheques?" I say. Amanda, my mother, and the girls have dropped me and my golf clubs at the front door; by now they are halfway to the zoo in Rome. I envision myself sitting in the dining room of one of the Ten Best Golf Clubs in Italy nursing a cappuccino for four hours, paid for with my last Euro. "We accept them, of course," the clerk says.

Out of my wallet I take the very same Travelers Cheques that no bank in Lecce would touch, and I hand them over to the two genial clerks behind the desk at one of the Ten Best Golf Clubs in Italy. First one man examines the cheques, then the other. "They are fine," the first one says. *Va bene'.* A great flood of relief goes through me. "The only problem is that these cheques are in dollars. We will have to calculate the exchange rate into Euros."

"Fine," I say, glancing at the clock behind him.

His colleague opens a drawer and takes out a calculator. The cost for a day of golf is sixty Euros (in order to play one of the ten best courses in America you would have to spend five times this sum). Sixty Euros, I know, from all the things we've paid for in the past three weeks, is, at the prevailing rate of exchange, approximately sixty-five dollars. I have given him a hundred dollars in cheques. He punches a set of numbers into the calculator, looks at the little screen, punches in another set, and says he owes me fifty dollars.

"Fine," I say. *Va bene.* Fifty, twenty, eighty-eight-oh-five, it doesn't matter to me. I want to finish a round of golf before the Kangoo reappears in the parking lot.

But his friend then looks over his shoulder and says, "No. Impossible." One must calculate the exchange rate, and then subtract the commission the bank charges for cashing Travelers Cheques.

"I think the exchange rate is about a Euro equals a dollar and ten cents," I say. "Why don't we just call it that?"

But they are studying the calculator as a team. More numbers get punched in. Both men frown.

I think: the same company that made your credit card machine made your calculator. But I do not say it.

"No, it can't be," the first man says.

"Of course. Look."

A third fellow in a sport coat appears behind the counter. Punches in some numbers. "With the commission," he says, "it will be seventy-nine dollars."

"Fine," I say. *Va bene'*. Fifty, seventy-nine, what difference does it make? I want to play golf.

They have accepted the Travelers Cheques and given me my change, when the third man says, "No, wait. We need to figure that again."

I am not joking here, and I am not exaggerating.

"Fine," I say. "While you are doing that, I'm going to call the *agriturismo* where we'll be staying tonight." One of the three mathematicians is kind enough to look up the number in the Olgiata Golf Club computer, and point me toward a pay phone in an alcove off the lobby. I dial the number and get a fax signal. At the start of the fax signal, I have more than three Euros left on my phone card, enough for something like a thirty-minute conversation. Five seconds later, at the end of the fax signal, I have nothing. Zero. Out of time.

I go back to the desk, where the calculations are still going on, and tell my friends that I think they accidentally gave me the fax number of the *agriturismo*. They apologize. They look up the correct number and let me use their phone. Two rings and Giampiero answers, owner of an *agriturismo* called Locanda Rosati, and a man we consider almost family. He remembers me immediately. "Tonight?" he says, after we've asked about each other's families. "Tonight we are closed, the restaurant is closed. Come stay, but . . . "

"Can you recommend a restaurant nearby?"

He hesitates for all of three seconds. "Listen, you come, we'll figure something out. We'll make something for you, a simple pasta. Do the girls eat pasta? Yes, of course, you just come and we'll figure everything out."

That done, I hang up the phone and return my attention to the small drama unfolding before me. I say, "I don't really care how much you charge me. I just want to play golf. My wife and children are going to Rome, they have left already in fact, going to the zoo, and they'll be back by—"

"One moment, one moment," the third one says. *Un attimo.*

In time, we settle on seventy dollars, I receive my change, and then walk all the way around the side of the building to the caddie master's shop, at which point I realize I have forgotten to pay for the golf cart. Usually I walk when I golf—the game was made for walking—but time is of the essence here. So I go back to the reception desk, we do some more calculations, I pay, locate my cart, load up my clubs, and am set free on the course.

It is a beautiful course, one of the Ten Best in Italy. Really. The Italian Open, a European Tour event, was held here a few years back, and the slick greens and difficult doglegs have the feel of a PGA tour venue. The day is warm, I am playing fairly well, knocking my Titleist along manicured fairways, past million-Euro homes. I sometimes think that people love golf so much because it requires one's full concentration. Everything else, every worry and dream, fades away and you're just there

193

on the course, calculating your distance, choosing your club, focusing on the ball, making your swing, watching your four-dollar Pro-V1 fly into the woods and ricochet around in the foliage. It's a solitary dance of concentration, a sort of mind-wash.

At the turn, a pretty young woman in a kiosk serves me a mozzarella and tomato sandwich and a cup of espresso, and then I am playing again, the back nine, gentle hills with old trees, small ponds, sand traps, flags waving lazily in the first breath of spring. There are Etruscan ruins by the side of the seventeenth hole, gravesites in a little burrow. I remember that, the last time I played Olgiata, I joined up with two Italian retirees, whacked an errant shot into one of these burrows, and declined, out of respect, to go in there searching for it. What did the Etruscan ghosts make of that, I wonder. But this time around I hit a near perfect approach shot into the difficult seventeenth green, then make a beautiful downhill putt for birdie. It's a nice way to end. Rather than keep the girls, Amanda, and my mother waiting, I decide to skip the last hole and hustle back to the clubhouse.

My traveling mates have had a nice day in Rome—a visit to the zoo, lunch with ice cream, no getting lost. I listen to their excited stories about a hippopotamus; they hear about my birdie putt. At peace, all of us, at peace at long last, we head up the highway toward Orvieto, and our favorite *agriturismo* in Italy.

31

There is, however, one small problem: After we've gone four or five kilometers beyond the gate of Olgiata, I look down at the gauge and see that there's not enough gas in the Kangoo's tank to get us where we're going. It is five o'clock on a Sunday night. On the highway north we turn into a gas station with a big metal OPEN sign out front. The sign is clanging in the wind. We stop, turn off the engine; I get out, insert the credit card, prepare to lift the nozzle and fill up. But nothing happens. Nothing registers on the pump. No little electronic message asking us to wait a minute, choose the octane, lift the nozzle. I look around for a few seconds, perplexed, try moving the handle this way and that. And then figure out what's wrong: the gas station is closed.

We go on, slowly, trying to stretch our fuel supply by gliding down the hills. We pass another gas station—OPEN—that turns out to be closed. A third gas station, same story. By now the needle is hard up against the red line and we're still fifty miles from Orvieto. But then our luck shifts: we approach a station that seems to be closed. On closer inspection, we see a Bangladeshi attendant standing out in the lot, a happy soul, a sort of angel in disguise. I think of the good wishes I sent down toward his countrymen, grilling their dinner in the courtyard behind our apartment in Lecce. Could this be some kind of payback from the universe? This black-haired young fellow has reincarnated here, south of Orvieto, for just long enough to fill the Kangoo with gas, and then he will ascend to the heavens where he belongs.

32

Orvieto is where the whole *agriturismo* fetish began. Five years earlier, Amanda and I arrived in Rome after a sleepless overnight flight. Alexandra was four months old, we were new at the job of being parents. At Fiumicino Airport we climbed into our rented car and headed north, toward the apartment we'd rented in Lucca, but by the time we reached the mountaintop town of Montefiascone we were too weary to go on, so we pulled into a parking area in the shadow of the domed cathedral there, and all three of us slept. We awoke at dusk, and got back on the road. But in a little while the lack of a real sleep caught up with us again, with Amanda and me at least, and, just as darkness was falling we saw a sign for an *agriturismo* and made the turn. We had never stayed at an *agriturismo* before, but a good friend of ours had, and her reports made us curious. The turn led us along a short driveway into a gravel parking area beside a restored Umbrian farmhouse, all brown stone, red tile roofs and window shutters. It turned out that this place was *Locanda Rosati*, which, we have since come to believe, is Italian for: "Come stay with us for a night and we will cure whatever ails you."

The rooms at *Locanda Rosati* are Zen rooms, with unvarnished pine furniture made by the Michaelangeli family in Orvieto. The furniture is decorated with wooden cutouts of frogs, porcupines, and foxes—each room has a particular animal as its mascot—the beds are covered in white linen with soft quilts, the windows look out on a swimming pool and olive trees, and the rolling hills of northern Umbria—the province referred to, in tourist literature, as "The Green Heart of Italy". On that first night the dinner was a five-course extravaganza served in a cavernous downstairs dining room, with bottles of wine lining the fieldstone walls, and logs blazing in the fireplace. Pasta, chicken *cacciatore*, salad, wine, cheese, fruit, dessert. The owners, Giampiero Rosati, his sister Alba, and her husband Paolo, sat at our table and talked with us as if we were family. We had a marvelous sleep. The next morning, we went downstairs to the now sunny dining room where, unsettled by the long flight perhaps, Alexandra threw up all over herself and Amanda. (What is it about Italy that turns our girls into Olympian vomiters?) Giampiero laughed, a father's laugh. I will never forget that laugh. *"Ah,"* he said gently, *"e' regurgitato tutto"*. She has thrown up everything. He brought us a towel, laughing quietly, as happy to help as if it were his own child. *E' regurgitato tutto.*

We sat there with Giampiero, Paolo and Alba, slathering homemade jam on slices of thick peasant bread, drinking the strong coffee with warm milk, and we were converts to the religion of *agriturismo*. This was the way to live.

We stopped at *Locanda Rosati* again, two years later, on an excursion north from Molly's apartment in Rome—more great food and warmth, more healing.

So now, with a full tank of gas, we make the last part of the drive to Orvieto, find the sharp left turn off highway 71, pull into the gravel lot, and feel almost as if we have arrived at the home of a favorite cousin. Giampiero hugs and kisses us, makes a huge fuss over the girls and my mother. Alba and her husband have "put something small together", on their day off, which means they have made us an incredible pasta with sweet plum tomatoes, followed by a rabbit and roast potato stew, with wine, bread, olives, and a *limoncello* . We talk with them for two hours—about their recent trip to India, about the government of Silvio Berlusconi, about the illnesses of children and the anxiety of parents. We look back in their guest book to find entries made on our previous two visits, show those historical scribblings to my mother and Alexandra, then make another entry, hoping we will be here again, showing what we now write to a more grown-up Juliana.

That night I'm awakened from a deep sleep by a shaft of moonlight that cuts through a small space in the shutters and rests, for a little while, exactly on my forehead. There can be no disputing that this is a light from heaven, beacon of my lost ancestors, warming me.

33

We are in the homestretch now. Two more nights on the road (I have the address of an *agriturismo* near La Spezia, on the Ligurian coast), a last night at the airport hotel Valter recommended, and we'll be leaving the *bel paese* more or less in one piece. At breakfast in *Locanda Rosati*—the same simple fare we always have here: fresh Tuscan bread with butter and jam, coffee with hot milk, slices of apple and pear—I check, double-check, and triple-check the description of the chosen *agriturismo* near La Spezia. I want this place to be exceptionally nice, the equal of *Locanda Rosati*, if such a thing is possible. I want us all to leave Italy on a happy note.

The only problem is that Amanda, who never complains about pain, and has been stoic about her back troubles over the past week, is worried about a badly aching, bloodshot eye. It must be that there is still some interest remaining on whatever karmic debt we have been paying off with our various health troubles on this trip. As we exchange kisses and embraces and promises to return with Giampiero, Alba, and Paolo, and then head north toward Prato, the pain in her eye gets worse. It has been very windy on this northward trip, just about every day, and we guess that something sharp has blown in and lodged beneath her eyelid. We stop in Prato for lunch in a little *osteria* run by a man with red hair. The food is disappointing and overpriced. During this lackluster meal, Amanda's eye situation gets so bad that we decide to stop into a *farmacia* after we've eaten. In Italy, the *farmacia*, plays a slightly different role than it does in America; you're more likely to go there for a dose of medical advice, along with your drugs. In the *farmacia* in Prato, we inquire of the three white-coated attendants who are talking with each other and sitting around looking bored. "Oh, no," one of them says when he hears the description of Amanda's troubles, "we can't help you with that. For that kind of thing you have to go to the emergency room. You don't want it to get infected."

But Amanda thinks it will eventually go away on its own, and says we should just head to La Spezia and not worry about it.

This is the description of the La Spezia *agriturismo* in our guide book: "*L'azienda e' immersa nel verde di frutteti e vigneti ed e' situata nel cuore della bassa Lunigiana a pochi chilometri dal mare. Nei dintorni e' possibile visitare broghi medioevali, castelli, pievi, cave di marmo, grotte, e terme.*" The establishment is immersed in the greenery of orchards and vineyards and is situated in the heart of the lower Lunigiana section, a few kilometers from the sea. In the surrounding area it is possible to visit medieval settlements, castles, country churches, caves of marble, grottoes and thermal baths."

Seems to fit the bill.

"Situated in the heart of the lower Lunigiana," proves to be the most accurate part of that description. So deep in the heart of the lower Lunigiana, in fact, that we have an amazingly difficult time finding the place. We don't get lost, exactly. We just can't find it. After climbing out of the little city of Aulla for what seems like half an hour, dutifully following the directions in the book, we come to a T in the road. We are looking for the village of Fivizzano. At this T, there is a sign pointing to the left that says: FIVIZZANO. But there is also a sign pointing to the right that says: FIVIZZANO.

"You should take a picture of that," I say to Amanda.

She nods, but makes no move to get out her camera.

"What do you think, Mum? Right to Fivizzano or left to Fivizzano?"

"Straight," my mother says. *"Sempre diritto."*

Even after all this long trip, my mother has retained her sense of humor: straight is over a cliff.

We go left. We climb along increasingly narrow roads into a tiny village—maybe it is Fivizzano, maybe not; maybe there are two Fivizzani—where a happy young man with a briefcase tells us the *agriturismo* we are looking for is only a short distance ahead. We drive the short distance. We see the signs. The signs encourage us to take a sharp right turn and the turn leads us down a road so steep it seems to be diving into a river valley between two mountainsides. It would not feel inappropriate to attach a parachute to the back of the Kangoo. On and on the road goes, down down down, the scenery absolutely spectacular, unearthly, as it rises around us: the snow-dusted mountains with forested hills bumping out from slanted slopes here and there, the cold blue river winding below, fields along its banks. But the road is endless. By the time we reach the *agriturismo*— the downhill road culminates in its driveway—I am low on patience and low on hope. "You go in," I say to Amanda. "I'm not sure what I'd do if we've come all this way and the rooms turn out to be no good."

Amanda is gone ten minutes. The kids, my mother, and I, sit in the car, stupefied by the long descent. I look at the odometer, which reads: 3673. Since the cool morning three weeks ago on which we picked up the Kangoo at the Malpensa airport, we have driven 2200 miles. Here, in the heart of the lower Lunigiana, it feels like we're breathing about half a mile below sea level. Amanda and I have been married a couple of decades; we know each other well. So, when she steps out of the stone house and into the sunlight, I can see instantly that we are in trouble.

"They don't take credit cards," she says. "And the rooms are . . . so-so. Why don't you come in and have a look, Rol?"

I don't need to go in and have a look. I am not interested in so-so, not for our last couple of nights in Italy. And, since they don't take credit cards and we, of course, don't have enough cash, we'll have to make the long long drive into Aulla and back, either tonight or tomorrow morning, and find another Bancomat. I shake my head. And there is no resistance.

This sad little interlude, this long drive for nothing, this decision not to settle for so-so in the lower Lunigiana, will turn out to be the definition of a blessing in disguise. But, at the moment, turning the car around in the parking lot beneath the world, 2200 miles on our odometer, the disguise is very convincing.

We climb and climb, retracing our route through what might or might not be one or the other of the Fivizzani. Back in Aulla we catch a big traffic delay as a freight train passes. I can feel the children's patience ticking like the mechanisms on small twin bombs. I want one break now, one last break, one good note on which they and my mother and Amanda and I can say farewell. But I'm getting some bad sounds on the intuition channel. Just when we thought we had bleached our shoes clean of the cause of our bad luck, a thin stink of misfortune has come seeping up through the dashboard all over again.

When the train finally passes and the clot of cars and trucks loosens, we find a phone booth and I call our backup *agriturismo*. The phone rings and rings, but I am not a soul who gives up easily. At last, a woman answers. No vacancy.

I call our second backup. The woman there sounds sweet and generous over the phone; the place sounds pretty good.

203

Then she begins to give directions. These are the directions I scribble down in the guidebook margins, printed here in their exact form, without embellishment: "Go into La Spezia, through the industrial zone, and follow signs for the Centro. Take a left at the fifth light. Take your second right. Go a hundred and fifty meters and you'll see another light. Take your second left after that light. Then take your second right after that. After the next light you will see a tunnel. Go left at the light before (?) The tunnel. Left at the next light. Then another left. You will see Carrello Street—"

At this point I am so far behind her that I stop writing down the directions. But the woman is not finished: "At the third light you will see a store. Opposite the store is a street called———. Make a sharp turn here. Go six more lights and take a left. Then your second right. Go through another tunnel and the road climbs into the hills. At the third right . . ."

I am leaning my head against the glass of the phone *cabine*, and I am saying *"Si, si,"* after each new turn, light, tunnel, cross street, and unmissable landmark. *"Si . . . si."* Finally, she stops and asks me if I've understood. I take a breath. "Listen," I say. "You are very kind. But we have gotten lost in Italy so many times on this vacation that I don't think we are going to make it. I don't think we could find your *agriturismo*. Really."

"No, no," she says. "It's not that difficult. We will come and pick you up at—"

"I'm sorry," I say. "If you don't see us by seven o'clock we aren't coming. We couldn't find it."

"But it's not difficult," she says, kindly, hopefully.

The phone card has eight seconds left on it. "I'm sorry," I manage to say once more, before the line clicks dead.

Walking out of the *cabine*, I feel an almost irresistible urge to fling the *Guida all' Agriturismo in Italia*, a nice, twenty-dollar, large-format, illustrated paperback, into the weeds at the side of the parking lot. The inhabitants of the Kangoo are hungry and tired. I open the door and feel the expectation in their faces. Four sets of hopeful eyes.

"No good," I say.

We drive on.

We head toward La Spezia. Darkness falls. We get stuck in traffic because there is some kind of holy-day festival going on in La Spezia. We are searching both sides of the street for hotels, but don't see any. Amanda tells me there's a hotel listed in another guidebook we sometimes use, but it is in Portovenere, thirty minutes north along the coast. So we head toward Portovenere in the darkness, on a winding road that runs on top of a cliff above the sea.

"Oh, no, my head hurts," Alexandra says.

Juliana is screaming for a digestive cracker.

My mother is silent.

Amanda has the guidebook on her lap and is studying it with what I recognize from her posture as a desperate optimism. On we go through the Italian darkness. Lights flicker in the bay to our left, far below.

We drive for the better part of half an hour and find the hotel Amanda saw in the guidebook, a place called the Belvedere, which is Italian for "nice view." I don't, at this point, care about the view, and can't see it in the dark in any case. I go in and check the place out. Elegant lobby. Two clean rooms with baths on the second floor, breakfast included. Excellent, fine, no problem. We park on the street and carry in some bags. Our two rooms have balconies, and televisions on which our president is giving the president of Iraq a forty-eight-hour ultimatum. We go out and have a delicious *pasta al pesto* with good wine in an upstairs restaurant, right on the shore of the Bay of Poets. I'm a literary man, and it pleases me to know that Byron and Shelley and D.H. Lawrence and Virginia Woolf and Dante hung out here, inspired by the razor-clam soup and the view. But it is too late now. Forty-eight hours left in Italy and I feel that, somewhere in the Lunigiana foothills, in the phone booth, on the mountain road, my love for traveling in this country has perished. Dead. Gone. *Finito.* Too much has happened, health-wise. There have been too many difficulties. We've gotten lost too many times. Too many things haven't worked out the way we wanted them to work out. My storage tank of travel patience has been depleted, and the gauge on the backup tank rests on the bad side of E.

34

If anything is capable of reviving that love it is the breakfast served at the Hotel Belvedere the following morning.
Food heals. At least some of the time. At least for me. The
view from the sunlit, window-walled breakfast room is out
over the shimmering Bay of Poets to the snow-capped peaks of
the Apuan Alps. The meal includes fresh croissants (we smell
them baking as we walk down the stairs and through the lobby), pumpernickel bread (my mother's favorite), the rich Italian
yogurt that tastes like it has been mixed with whipped cream,
fresh pears and apples, peach and orange juice, eggs, cereal, the
wonderful strong coffee served in individual aluminum coffee-
pots with a separate pot of hot milk. The sun is pouring in. Juliana woke up screaming in the middle of the night, but whatever was troubling her was short lived, a bad dream maybe, and
she is fine now. From where we sit we can look straight down
on a playground by the shore. Perfect.

Except that Amanda's eye is swollen. As we finish breakfast, her usually sunny morning mood is subdued. From the
genial, bewigged clerk at the Belvedere's front desk, we get the
name of a doctor. Alexandra climbs up on my back, Juliana
rides the stroller. Loaded down with diaper bags, camera bags,
and the assorted other paraphernalia of the domestic caravan,
three generations of Merullos go out into the sunlit Ligurian
morning and turn left, down the street, toward the town center.

Before we reach the doctor's office, I see an ambulance parked at the side of the road, and three orange-booted attendants standing around. There is a door with *Pronto Soccorso* on it (to my ear at least, this sounds nicer than "First Aid"). I ask about seeing a doctor, and one of the attendants waves us through that door.

Inside, it is difficult to get the lay of the land. We have stumbled into a sort of blunt hallway—an elevator directly in front of us, an unmarked door a few feet to our left, and a staircase winding up to the right. It seems to be some kind of public clinic, for the poor perhaps. But there are no signs. As we are wondering what to do, an old man who looks like he's spent the night on the street shuffles past us, and goes through the door.

"There's your doctor," I say quietly to Amanda.

"Really?" my mother asks.

"No, just joking, Ma. A bad joke. I'm getting sarcastic these days. I'm burnt out. Sorry."

In a moment the door opens and the old fellow who just shuffled past waves us in. He is the doctor.

Past his prime maybe. With the splotched skin of someone who has seen too much sun, or too much drink, or too many troubles, or all of the above. But this is a good doctor—confident, gentle, no-nonsense. He speaks to us, however, in *extremely* measured Italian: *"E'. . . possibile,"* he tells me, after examining Amanda's eye and ascertaining that I speak better Italian than she does, *"che . . . qual . . . cosa . . .* It . . . could . . . be . . . that . . . some . . . thing . . . hard . . . do you understand? *Duro . . .* something *duro . . .* has . . . lodged . . . there. Do you understand? . . . *Duro."*

I tell him I understand fine.

"A . . . small . . . piece . . . of . . . glass . . . or . . . metal . . . or . . . stone. Who knows what it could be? Do you understand?"

"*Sì, capito.*"

"*Bene'.* Now . . . I . . . am . . . going . . . to . . . put . . . some . . . anesthetic . . . drops . . . in . . . the . . . eye . . . of . . . your . . . spouse."

He sounds as if he is asking permission to undress her. Fine, I say. *Capito.* No problem. It's just drops, right?

"*Sì.*" He goes on at the same pace, perhaps a bit slower even. "These . . . . . . are . . . . . . just . . . . . . anesthetic . . . . . . drops . . . . . . For . . . . . . the . . . . . . pain. If there is something hard lodged there, these drops will do no good. Understand?"

"Yes."

"Now, if her condition does not improve, she will have to go to the hospital in La Spezia. I am a generalist, not a specialist. Your spouse will have to go to an eye specialist, do you understand?"

"*Sì.*"

"There . . . . . . is . . . . . . only . . . . . . one . . . . . . hospital . . . . . . there." He holds up one unsteady finger and twirls his wrist. "Ask anyone where it is and they will tell you. Only one."

"I understand."

Looked at from a distance of a few days, this whole scene, the last strange thirty-six hours or so, will take on a different meaning. The doctor's deliberateness in speaking to us, his mention of the hospital in La Spezia and the fact that it was the only hospital there, and the nearest one; the strange dive into the *agriturismo* in the valley and our decision to turn around and come back . . . in a day or so all of this will look like some kind of convoluted blessing. But of course we don't know that then.

With shaking hands the doctor opens a little kit. He starts to take out a sharp item, some kind of scalpel, then realizes his mistake and reaches for a dropper instead. This does not inspire much confidence, but I like the man, and more or less trust him. With shaking hands he tilts Amanda's head back, then holds the dropper an inch above her eye and lets fall two pale globes of liquid. He wipes his hands, washes them, and touches Amanda and then me on the shoulder with a gesture of pure grace.

We thank him four times. "What do we owe you?" I ask. *"Cuanto dobbiamo?"*

And he says, as if pleased to see that I am picking up the language, *"Niente.* Nothing. You owe me nothing. You can make a donation if you'd like."

I leave a ten-dollar bill on the table in the hall and we go out in search of the playground.

35

Along the curl of Portovenere's shore is a mile-long row of shops and restaurants and a promenade that climbs to a small stone church on a promontory overlooking the water. There are yellow tulips on the plain altar of this church, and sunlight pouring in on them, and a plaque on the wall stating that Napoleon's troops once set the roof and walls on fire because this was a bivouac for the Austro-Russian militia. Long before Napoleon's time, it was a place of pagan worship. Alexandra and I climb steps to a stone patio above, and look northeast along the rugged coastline that leads to the Cinque Terre, then southwest across the Bay of Poets to the mountains we can see from our hotel. Down below, my mother is pushing the sleeping Juliana back and forth in the stroller, in the warm sun. Amanda is shooting photographs. Another plaque commemorates Lord Byron's swim across this bay, and that strikes me as a strange and marvelous thing—the poet showing his physical side, spectators on the cliffs watching the famous man go. The sun is a warm, Mediterranean sun, a hint of summer in it. I want to take a swim myself, so much so that, later, Alexandra and I will shock the locals by wading knee-deep into the ice-water off the town beach.

We find a place for lunch and the waiter there decides not to charge us for the wine. We spend some time at the playground, some time walking around looking for souvenirs. "We should have come here right from the beginning," my mother says. "We should have just come to this place and stayed here."

She's right. One good decision like that would have saved us so much trouble. I put my arm around her shoulders and don't tell her that, on our first day in Italy, on our way to Pietrasanta from the airport in Milan, we passed within about six miles of this place.

We go back to the Belvedere to rest up and take in the war preparations on the TV. We finish the chest PT, dress up for dinner. Just before we leave, just at sunset, a full moon rises beyond the Apuan Alps and, in that ethereal light, Amanda shoots a picture of the girls on the balcony, Alexandra leaning her head down sideways toward her little sister, both of them in their best dresses. It will turn out to be one of those photographs that become a sort of landmark in the life of a family; it will be framed and stand prominently displayed on a Massachusetts side table for years and years.

That night, the restaurants along the promenade below our hotel are closed. I am not sure why. Because it is Tuesday, maybe. We wander around in the dark town and eventually find a place that's open, but the food there is strictly so-so, and a couple is smoking very close to us. I go through the by-now-familiar routine of getting up and approaching them and, as politely as I can, asking them if they would mind putting out their cigarettes, just for a few more minutes until we finish our meal, because of my daughter's health, and so on. This time, the little speech does not go over very well. Not well at all, in fact. The woman gives me the Evil Eye.

The Evil Eye is a southern Italian superstition: someone can look at you a certain way, with a certain bad intent, and put a curse on you. To this day, in Italian sections of American cities, you see men wearing chains around their necks with small gold peppers attached to them. This is not some kind of phallic food-fetish, but a lucky charm said to provide protection against the Evil Eye. In a strange way, this superstition is at the root of Italian generosity, since, in the small impoverished villages of southern Italy, anyone who had some good fortune was obliged to share it or risk the envy of the town, and with that envy, a good chance of falling victim to the Evil Eye.

I don't wear a necklace, and don't have any gold peppers.

With some reluctance, they extinguish their cigarettes, but it is too late. The damage has been done. A curse has been laid across me and my progeny, and, somehow, through some ancient blood-understanding, I know this. This time I don't go up to the waitress and leave her money so she can serve the couple a free liqueur when we're gone. We just finish our meal and go out and take a stroll in the dark town. At some point there, Alexandra loses her Barbie scarf. This is a tiny strip of gray cloth, a few inches long, easily replaceable, but she is distraught, inconsolable; the Evil Eye is starting to have its effect. We stand on the promenade listening to her wails echo off the old houses there. I remember what this is like. I remember the way, in the life of a small child, an ordinary object can take on magical power. So I hoist her up onto a spinal column that is missing one disc at belt level and broken in one place at heart level, and we retrace our steps on a Quixotic attempt to find a dark-colored scrap of cloth, in the dark town paved with dark stone. We make a large circle from the restaurant, up a long incline past other shops and eateries, Alexandra's tears dripping down inside my collar. On the point of surrender, we go through an archway and down a long dark set of stairs. And there, by some odd magic, as we are halfway down the stairs, Alexandra still on my back, I look down and see a tiny shadow near my shoe. Barbie's scarf.

We go back to the hotel and try to sleep. And we do sleep. We sleep quite well, in fact . . . until two-thirty in the morning, when Juliana wakes up screaming. There is something fundamentally different about the sound of this screaming: it's not her usual, middle-of-the-night bad moment. Amanda brings her into the bed with us and from four feet away I can feel the heat radiating from her body.

"She's burning up," Amanda says. She has packed a thermometer (the type of thing I tease her about in America, while we are preparing, and then thank her for later). Juliana has a temperature of 103.6, and is writhing and kicking and screaming in the bed with us in a way that is terrifying and strange. It is a kind of febrile hysteria. In a minute and a half, Amanda and I are up, awake, and fully dressed. She bundles up Juliana, forces a dose of liquid ibuprofen down her throat. I scribble a note and slip it under the door of the room beside ours, where Alexandra and my mother are sleeping. We hurry down the wide, curving, marble stairs into the lobby.

There is no one at the desk. I pound on the locked door behind the desk. No one answers. We walk through the lobby and the breakfast room. I go out onto the sidewalk and ring the bell but no one answers the bell. We call out—no answer. Which would not be anything to worry about except that, as I know it will, the front door of the hotel locks tight when I pull it closed.

The Evil Eye.

By the time we are on the mountain road that leads along the ragged coast from Portovenere to La Spezia, offering up prayers of thanks that we didn't decide to stay in the deep valley, the ibuprofen has kicked in and Juliana's mood has changed from hysterical to giddy. She has stopped screaming. She is counting, joyfully, almost raucously: Wan, thoo, fee. We are singing "Bah Bah Black Sheep" along with the tape, loudly, but her good mood feels too good and we know it won't last.

The road is empty, a fifteen-mile serpentine chute that

flings us into the sleeping city of La Spezia, where there . . . . . .
is . . . . . . only . . . . . . one . . . . hospital and everyone knows
where it is. It is three-thirty, the heart of the night. There are
signs for the *centro*, which we follow, but no signs for *ospedale*.

At last, after searching the streets for ten minutes, we see a
young couple coming arm-in-arm along the sidewalk, looking
as though they're on their way home from a bar, bathed in the
anticipation of some late-night lovemaking. We pull up beside
the young man, Amanda rolls her window down, and I lean
across and ask how to get to the hospital. He looks at Juliana in
her car seat in back, looks at Amanda's face, looks across at
me, and gives us careful, quick directions that go this way:
"That's a one-way street over there, see? But don't worry about
it at this hour. Go the wrong way down that one-way street and
through the tunnel, which is also one-way. The cars come the
other way, but don't worry, at this time of night there is not
much traffic. As soon as you come out of the tunnel, take a
right and you'll see the signs for the hospital."

Good directions, at last, and when we need them most.
And, in spite of everything, or maybe because of everything, I
get a small thrill out of driving into a dark tunnel the wrong
way. In three minutes we are at the hospital, driving up the
ramp to the emergency room, carrying Juliana into a plain-
looking peeling-paint room with two rows of plastic chairs facing an interior window. Two people are waiting there. They see
that we're carrying a sick young child and they wave us toward
the glass, ahead of them. I speak into the glass, get as far as,
"temperature of forty degrees" and we are waved through a
side door into the emergency room itself.

There, Juliana attracts a small audience of admirers. While
the doctor is examining her, and trying to make sense of my
broken-Italian explanation (she had a little pneumonia just before we left, and our doctor in America said it wasn't anything

that should keep us home and he gave her a five-day course of Zithromax. But after three days we were in Italy and she was throwing up so she had to stop taking it. We went to the hospital in Rome for the stomach flu, and there, etcetera etcetera) one of the pretty young nurses, who bears an eerie resemblance to my cousin Lenore, takes a surgical glove, blows it up into a five-fingered balloon, ties it off at the wrist, and draws a smiley face on it with blue marker. Juliana holds onto this lucky charm as if it is protection against the Evil Eye. With her other hand she is pushing a digestive cracker into her mouth, exhibiting about a hundredth as much anxiety as her Mom and Dad. But her face is flushed and her eyes glassy. The hospital is nothing like the gleaming place we took her to in Rome, with computers beeping and physicians hurrying this way and that. Here, the walls need paint, and you don't see a lot of fancy machinery; the whole place seems like a stage set for some World-War-II-vintage film. You expect to see soldiers with bloody bandages being carried down the halls on military stretchers. But there is also a general sense of competence and warmth that you don't always get in big city hospitals. We start to relax.

Once the first exam is finished, we are led—by an ambulance attendant so perfectly movie-star cool that he could take his orange boots and dark glasses and proud walk and start a rock and roll band—through a labyrinth of corridors, up an elevator, and to the pediatric ward, where Juliana is seen by another doctor. This woman puts a special diaper on her, makes her laugh. We carry her into a playroom where she immediately starts taking toys off the shelves and building a little world for herself. Amanda and I pace, watching her carefully, trying to get the sound of her screaming out of our ears. After a time the doctor checks her again, takes off the diaper and does some tests on the urine she's collected. There are white blood cells in the urine, and we're told that kids with urinary

216

infections often spike high fevers. Given the range of possibilities, this is not bad news. The doctor writes out a prescription, and then gives us a first dose of the antibiotic so we won't have to drive all over La Spezia at four a.m. looking for the twenty-four-hour *farmacia*.

No charge, again. We spread thank-yous around like ten-dollar tips at a fancy golf course. Juliana is sleepy now; we are exhausted. We pack her into the car and Amanda talks to me all the way along the dark mountain road home so I don't fall asleep at the wheel and send us plummeting down into the Bay of Poets. We talk about the sounds Juliana was making, about the nice people at the hospital, the nurse who looked so much like Lenore. It is our way of reweaving the torn fabric of our friendship, and by the time we get back to the curb in front of the Belvedere, all is more or less well.

We're worried about getting back into the hotel: it's four-forty-five and the town is asleep. But the front door is unlocked now, a mystery. We go past the unoccupied desk, climb the wide staircase and fall into an exhausted sleep.

<u>36</u>

In Italian, the word for "enough" is *basta*, and that's what I'm thinking when I wake up the next morning and stand tiredly at the balcony window, looking out at the spectacular view. *Basta*. That is the word that echoes in my thoughts as we enjoy a second Belvedere breakfast. Juliana is a bit sluggish, but it is the sluggishness of someone who has not slept enough, nothing more. Alexandra insists on spreading the butter on her croissant without assistance, and, when she finishes eating she traipses across the room to talk with an older woman in a wheelchair. A lush, summery sunlight falls through the windows on the pair of them. I have the sense that this woman has been coming to the Belvedere for many seasons, that she stayed here in her youth, her early married and mothering years, then middle age, late middle age, and now near the very end. I don't know why I have this sense; something in the way the waiters treat her, in the way she looks out at the view, then down at our happy daughter—as if she rolls her chair and her pain through swirls of pleasant memories, as if she knows what it feels like to have time slip out from beneath her, as if she is seeing something of herself, some beautiful spark, in our brown-eyed girl. They have a connection, she and Alexandra. My mother watches them. Amanda looks over. We have a flicker of wanting to stay.

But the tickets have been changed, we need to be heading

off to Milano. Amanda's back is no better so I lug the suitcases down the stairs and arrange them just so in the back of the Kangoo. *Basta*, I'm thinking, in spite of the nice moment at breakfast. *Basta*.

We loop down around the not very steep hairpin turn and stop for a while at the playground there, a few yards from the water. Amanda and I are barely awake, less attentive than usual. Juliana falls backwards off the two-foot-high stone wall at the edge of the playground and bumps her head. *Basta*.

We make the same drive we made the night before, down the long mountain road and then through the traffic-choked festivities in La Spezia. *Basta così*.

Italy is such a wonderful place to visit—why else would millions of tourists come here to spend their money and vacation time every year? A sunny, mountainous peninsula full of magnificent art, history, spectacular architecture, tremendous food, nice people. But I am done visiting here for a while, I can feel that in my bones. Later this same afternoon we will get lost again on the Autostrada leading out of Genoa and spend two hours more on the road than we need to. We will race across the unappealing plain near Milano with motorcycles and trucks buzzing and roaring around us, changing lanes, flashing their lights. We will find the hotel that Valter from Renault recommended on that first cool morning, near the airport, and be driven from there to a restaurant by a man who ignores red lights, then serves us a wonderful meal of lamb and lentils with polenta, in his own little place in the industrial wastelands near Malpensa. But it will be too late then.

At the airport, on the following morning, we will be run through a gamut of imbecilic bureaucracy—a woman at the Al Italia desk taking my credit card and, as expected, putting a thousand dollar charge on it because we are going home six days earlier than planned, and then writing out the code for the changed tickets, very slowly, twenty-three numbers, five times, while I wait to board. We will be shuttled from one desk to another—for the ticket change, for the suddenly oversized golf bag. The window seats we reserved will not have been saved for us. The clerk will wonder aloud if Juliana should have her own seat, though I've told her, twice now, that she already does. We will not be able to get to the second floor of the terminal to buy souvenirs because the elevators don't go to the second floor, for security reasons, though it is perfectly acceptable to take the stairs there, if you can manage to carry all your bags. We will, eventually, get on the plane and have a smooth flight home, just as the bombs begin falling on Iraq.

But before all this transpires, as we are driving north from Portovenere on a few hours sleep, with my mother and Alexandra playing poker in the back seat, and Juliana asleep there, we stop in the small city of Santa Margherita for lunch. Amanda and I and her sister Sarah once spent a very nice week in Santa Margherita, years ago, before the girls were born. We stayed in a simple hotel high up on a hillside, looking down past plane trees to the Ligurian Riviera. We had a string of good breakfasts in the hotel dining room, took walks, swam, sampled a dozen local restaurants, hiked overland to Portofino and lost ourselves in an olive grove on the way back. The memories are good. Amanda thinks we should make it farther up the highway before stopping—we still have a long ride to Milan ahead of us, after all—and she's probably right, but I want to stop in Santa Margherita for lunch, that's all. I am a man who has already broken up with his lover, the *bel paese*, and I'm looking for one last kiss by which to remember her.

And I get that kiss. The small city of Santa Margherita has been a fishing village since the twelfth century. It sits on a perfect curl of bay, just south of its more famous neighbor Portofino, and just north of Rapallo, where Ezra Pound liked to hang out, and where James Joyce once visited him. We find Santa Margherita without a single problem, remembering the roads and buildings, remembering the way sunlight reflects off the water and up against the hillsides just to the east, the way the buildings are painted with false windows, stones, and pillars, beautifully done.

We find a parking spot. I ask a kiosk attendant about a place to eat. He is playing solitaire on his computer, but steps out of the kiosk and tells us about a restaurant where he and his friends like to go, not touristy, not far, very good. Pezzi, it is called.

For half an hour we walk back and forth along the sunny promenade, working up an appetite, admiring the expensive sailboats rocking in the harbor, looking at the elegant old hotels set on manicured grounds, surrounded by palm trees and gravel paths. We walk to Pezzi, where the people seem happy to see us. They clear a table, they wait on us with a plainspoken intimacy I love—no false kindness here; no "Hi, my name is Eric and I'll be your server today." They bring a carafe of very good white wine. We have spaghetti with the creamy pesto sauce, a local delicacy, that we remember so well from our previous visit. We have onions stuffed with seasoned bread crumbs. We have a sweet vegetable soup that my mother especially enjoys, chocolate cake, coffee enough to keep us awake during the long ride to Milan.

The girls are happy and well. The food is succulent. The toilets have seats. We watch the happy bustle of the Italian lunch hour, waiters and waitresses bantering with their customers, plates and bowls of steaming food being carried out of the kitchen. I feel, as I sometimes do in Italy, a strange connection with the ancient past, and a link to my truest self.

My mother and I have had a little running joke going during this adventure. When the worst moments have safely passed, I turn to her and say, "Ma."

And she answers: "What, Rol?"

"Next year." I pause. "Florida."

But now, leaving Pezzi and strolling past a five-hundred-year-old church in the curving little shop-lined streets behind Santa Margherita's boulevard (is this the kind of thing you find in Fort Lauderdale?), I recall, in my bones and blood and belly, why I fell in love with this country in the first place. And for a little while, in spite of everything that has happened in the past few weeks, I nurture a fantasy of coming back the following spring, just as the sea turns warm enough for swimming. I will rent out two adjacent rooms in one of these graceful old hotels, spend a month here with the four people I care about most on this earth, eating, playing golf, swimming, taking walks up into the hillsides where people have been growing olives and grapes for thousands of years, where men and women have wanted to make themselves and their children and parents and wives and husbands happy, done everything in their power to carry them through a long winter on the sled of some shining, warm, impossible dream. I think about them, about us. I take a last sip of wine, and we head out into the Italian day.

EPILOGUE

Almost three years have passed now since our adventure in Contigliano and Lecce and, still, writing about that trip I can feel the particular kind of pain you feel when you've expended a lot of time, effort, and money on a vacation and it turns into a disaster. It's almost always the case with me that bad travel memories get washed away by the good, but not this time. With the clear vision of hindsight I can see the foolish decisions we made, large and small. We should have waited a month and gone someplace warmer. We should probably have rented a house from a person who had young children of her own, and understood their particular requirements. Maybe we should have stayed in Lecce another week, soaked up the sun, spent our money on the palatial apartment instead of on airplane ticket fees.

For the past couple of years we've escaped the Massachusetts winter by going—where else?—to Florida, and those vacations have been without incident: great weather, good food, a little golf, some beach time. Despite our particular health concerns, I feel that we're an exceptionally lucky family. We can afford these trips, both in terms of money, time, and school situation, and all three generations get along famously well.

Even so, as the weather gets cold again in this part of the world, and both the days and the options for entertainment shrink, I admit to feeling the tug of Italy again. The quality of the food, the emphasis on personal warmth, the feeling of being surrounded by ancient architectural masterpieces, the sense of history—you can't really put all that together in a single American vacation package. At least we've never been able to do that. Not long ago I got out an old Italian language textbook and put it on the bedside table. I've started checking the weather reports from Genoa. Amanda and I talk about the possibility of making another trip, in a year or two maybe, when the girls are a bit older. After all, we survived the previous one, didn't we? And, as I always say: you take a trip to learn something about yourself, not necessarily to have a good time.

There is still so much to learn.

The End
Conway 4.17.03—11.29.05

AFTERWORD

Dear Readers,

As you can tell from the dates at the end of the epilogue—
4.17.03—11.29.05—I started *Taking the Kids to Italy* not long
after we returned from our disastrous Italian vacation, and
worked on it, sporadically, over a period of two and a half
years. It was, for me, an exercise in healing, an attempt to shine
a humorous light on what had been one of the roughest
months of our lives to that point. Once the manuscript was
finished, the pages sat around in a drawer in my writing room
until PFP Publishing contacted me and asked if I had anything
they might serialize in the monthly newsletter they put out via
RolandMerullo.com. I mentioned that I had this unpublished
travel memoir from an old vacation. The people at PFP read it,
liked it, and began including a chapter in each month's newsletter. The response has been so enthusiastic that they decided to
bring the whole story out as a book, in paperback and eBook
formats, so here it is.

I know, of course, that there are worse things in life than a
vacation that goes all wrong. Many of those things can't be
made funny, no matter from what angle you view them. But I
hope I've made our 2003 Italian struggles into a story that pro-
vides a few moments of comic relief for readers and gives
more evidence of the universality of the human experience. We
all love, argue, endure difficulties, cherish dreams, and if writing—perhaps travel writing especially—isn't about demonstrat-
ing that connection, then why tell the story? Yes, it was a difficult time, but we all survived. My mother, over ninety now, still
likes to spend time with us and talks about joining us for another trip one day soon. Amanda and I celebrated our 34th

wedding anniversary last month, and still share a love of travel. Remarkably enough, our daughters, now sixteen and twelve, still seem to enjoy taking trips with their parents, and joke with us about how easily a dreary winter day can lead to a breakfast-table conversation, that leads to plans being made for another adventure, that leads to the purchase of plane tickets and the making of hotel reservations.

We've been to Italy twice more since the Contigliano trip. In 2007 we spent a summer at Lake Como—probably the best vacation we've ever had—a trip that formed the basis for another book, *The Italian Summer*, which focuses more on golf and eating. And in 2009, we drove from Genoa to Orvieto to Venice, spending time at some fine *agriturismos*, getting lost slightly less often, meeting a lot of friendly people and seeing some beautiful sights. None of us fell ill on any of these trips. There was no vomiting, no infected eyes, no bruised skulls from nighttime falls onto stone floors. Maybe we packed all our bad luck into the trip described in these pages. I hope so, because, if we can somehow find the financial means to do it, we all want to go back to Italy again soon.